1960

This book may be kept

PRACTICE AND THEORY OF
PROBATION AND PAROLE

PRACTICE AND THEORY OF

PROBATION
AND
PAROLE

BY DAVID DRESSLER

1959

COLUMBIA UNIVERSITY PRESS, NEW YORK

So many people have meant so much. Intimations of mortality suggest I shall never be able to dedicate a book to each. This one, therefore, is for Belle, David Mark, Joshua, Sylvia, H. Louise, Brownie, Steve, and Anne.

PREFACE

When, in 1951, I wrote *Probation and Parole,* it was intended
as a rationale of the field and not as a textbook. Since then, as
was to be expected, my thinking has changed somewhat. In
part, this is due to the fact that, farther removed from the field,
I am able to view it more objectively, from the vantage point
of a college campus. The man in the field sometimes cannot
see the forest for the trees. The academician, of course, may
not see individual trees, only forest. I have tried, in this volume,
to see trees and forest. I may not have succeeded but I have
attempted to survey both practice and theory and to place
them in perspective.

This is not, however, a rewrite of the earlier book. It is
planned as a text for college courses in probation and parole;
as a secondary source for courses in criminology and juvenile
delinquency; a handbook for in-service training in correctional
agencies; and as one man's rationale of the field, addressed to
persons currently in practice.

Because I have tried to reach somewhat disparate groups,
certain chapters may be elementary for some readers. Others
may question the inclusion of probation and parole history.
I believe there is reason for it. To appraise modern practice,
one must examine its philosophical roots and historical origins.
Moreover, the history of probation and parole rarely is found
in one place in the existing literature. I felt there would be
utility in assembling the piecemeal data in one volume.

The detailed material on laws relating to probation and parole and the present status of these services in the country at large may bore the experienced worker. If so, I apologize. It was my thought that even though these readers will find some of the data elementary, something might yet be gained by setting them into one frame and viewing them in the whole.

I owe thanks to many for their help. Sol Rubin, counsel of the National Probation and Parole Association, was good enough to go over part of the manuscript. He did so with meticulous care, eliminating error and updating me with regard to law and present status of probation and parole operations. He is probably the outstanding authority on these subjects, and I am deeply grateful that he found time to assist me. Beyond checking my manuscript he was generous enough to make available some of his own, as yet unpublished, manuscript material on the subject.

Richard A. McGee, Director of the California Department of Corrections, was equally gracious and painstaking in evaluating portions of the volume. The critique by one of the nation's most progressive and creative administrators helped reorient me on several subjects.

My good friend Dr. Walter M. Wallack, Warden of Wallkill State Prison in New York State, cheerfully helped with another segment of the book, and I am indebted to him not only for this but for the stimulation he has been to me in general and for the encouragement he has given me over the years.

My sincere thanks to Ernest W. Witte, Executive Director, and Ann Elizabeth Neely, Consultant on Program Services, both of the Council on Social Work Education, for extremely valuable information on the training and backgrounds of correctional workers and other aspects of staffing and personnel practice.

Members of faculties in California and elsewhere have been helpful, and to them my gratitude: Dr. Vernon Fox, Florida State University; Hugh P. O'Brien, University of Notre Dame;

Dr. Dorothy Zietz, Sacramento State College; Dr. Richard O. Nahrendorf, Los Angeles State College; Dr. Frank M. Boolsen, Fresno State College; Dr. David S. Milne, San Diego State College; Dr. T. C. Esselstyn, San Jose State College.

I wish to emphasize, however, that while those mentioned were generous of their time and kind enough to present their thinking, I must take full responsibility for everything in this volume. The opinions I express are my own, and not necessarily theirs. Undoubtedly, some of my views run counter to those of the people who were kind enough to assist me.

To Sylvia Jaffe and H. Louise Van Valkenburg, a very special thank you. My very dear friends, whom I shall always regard with affection, they not only stood for my editing and reediting and editing the editings, but for me, too, in the process.

DAVID DRESSLER

Van Nuys, California

CONTENTS

PRACTICE AND THEORY OF
PROBATION AND PAROLE

1

TOWARD AN UNDERSTANDING OF
PROBATION AND PAROLE

In 1883, Eliza M. Mosher, M.D., presented a paper before the National Conference of Charities and Corrections in which she asserted: "Justice demands that offenders against law shall be punished! Christianity demands for them a discipline which shall correct and reform their evil natures, changing them from criminals to God-fearing, law-abiding citizens." Prison life, she advised, "must be made laborious, exacting, constraining, and the prisoner . . . must not forget that 'the way of the transgressor is hard.'"[1] Eliza was harsher than Miss E. A. Hall who, at the same gathering, urged that "criminal girls" in correctional institutions be supervised by friendly, warm-hearted women "who have faith in them." She suggested such girls be placed "in the midst of proper books and papers, flowers, pictures, music and home industries. These create a desire for a permanent home, with good, upright friends and all that pertains to it."[2]

The two statements reflect the old and the new of that period. Here is opinion in evolution. The middle of the nineteenth century had seen the dawn of an era of penal reform. Several

[1] Eliza M. Mosher, M.D., "Discipline in Prisons," in *Proceedings, Tenth Annual National Conference of Charities and Corrections, 1883* (Madison, Wis.: Midland Publishing Co., 1884), pp. 211–16.
[2] E. A. Hall, "Reformation of Criminal Girls," in *ibid.*, pp. 188–99.

decades later, the conservatives were still holding to their ideas, but marked gains had been made in reorienting correctional philosophy. To understand present-day probation and parole it is necessary to examine this period of ferment.

The Evolution of Correctional Thought

It was no accident that correctional thought turned in new directions in the nineteenth century. This was an age of intellectual adventure, of consequent social change. Darwin had stunned the world with *Origin of Species*. Huxley and Spencer adapted his theories to social phenomena which, they suggested, were an outgrowth of forces that could be discovered and understood. In the decade 1850–60, thinkers applied the scientific method to the investigation of culture and society. They wanted to know why human beings behave as they do, what produces social problems, how they might be alleviated. Everywhere, man wanted to know *why* and *how*.

Darwinism was itself an outgrowth of social ferment, while at the same time contributing to it. This was the era of agitation for woman suffrage, temperance reform, labor organization, a time when "restless sap flowed in the veins of . . . people and they took up their beds and walked." [3] Gold was discovered in California. The westward movement was on. Alaska was purchased. Technological changes occurred almost daily. The first underwater cable, between Governor's Island and Castle Garden, off New York, was laid in 1842. The first message over the first telegraph line was transmitted in 1844. A railroad train crossed the Mississippi in 1856.

Governmental systems were reappraised. The doctrine of the divine right to rule was attacked. Louis Philippe was dethroned. Ferdinand I of Austria abdicated the same year, and there were revolts in Ireland, Lombardy, Venice, Denmark,

[3] Meade Minnegerode, *The Fabulous Forties* (New York: G. P. Putnam's Sons, 1924), pp. v–vi.

and Schleswig-Holstein. Garibaldi unified Italy by revolt in 1860. Emperor Maximilian of Mexico was executed in 1867. The Orient too felt the impact of the times. Feudalism was abrogated in Japan and a constitution promulgated in 1889.

The abolitionist tracts and *Uncle Tom's Cabin,* published in 1852, inflamed the minds of men against the institution of slavery, and this may have had its effect upon penological thought. Walt Whitman created a new poetry form in volumes like *Leaves of Grass,* published in 1855. And—the very wonder of wonders—in 1869 the territory of Wyoming granted the franchise to that frail vessel, woman.

While heavily tinctured with older, more traditional ideas and attitudes, this was above all a cycle in world history in which humanitarianism came to the front. Belief in the dignity of man, respect for his personality, were borrowed from the Bible and translated into a code of behavior. The more brutal and denigrating sections of the English Poor Laws were in process of amendment. There was still a highly moralistic cast to the giving of charity, but change was in the making and Lady Bountiful was being replaced by the professional social worker.

Humanitarianism made itself felt in the United States when, in 1857, the first municipal pension fund was established, providing disability and death benefits for New York City policemen. Six years later, the first state board of charities was founded, in Massachusetts. In 1869, in the same state, this country saw its first state board of health.

Private industry was affected too. In 1875 the first private pension plan in American industry was instituted.

In this yeasty atmosphere, criminology and penology rose to new levels. The decline of the classical school of criminology marked this change. A hundred years before, Beccaria suggested that the way to attack crime was to change laws, not men. Would you prevent crime, he asked?

Let the laws be clear and simple; let the entire force of the nation be united in their defence; let them be intended to favour every individual, than any particular classes of men; let the laws be feared, and the laws only. The fear of the law is salutary.[4]

Beccaria held that the criminal code should specify a given penalty for a particular crime. Judges should mete out an identical sentence for each occurrence of the same offense. Beccaria aimed to eliminate preferential treatment in court. He believed certainty of justice would act as a deterrent to crime. We know today that there is no such thing as the "same" crime, hence the theory of equal penalties scarcely applies. Two men may commit what the code calls burglary, but each act will in some way be different from the other.

The intent of the perpetrator was of no concern to the courts, Beccaria insisted. "They err, therefore, who imagine that a crime is greater, or less, according to the intention of the person by whom it is committed . . ."[5] Today the intent of the offender is of vital concern.

It was to be expected, in an era in which men were leaning toward humanitarianism, that doctrines such as Beccaria's would be rebutted. Where the classical school emphasized law, humanitarians concentrated on man. The offender rather than the offense became the center of interest. The new criminologists deplored institutions that did no more than incarcerate and punish. They advocated programs that would help prisoners change. Some of their ideas, viewed today, appear naïve and weighted with undue faith in the moral lecture, but for their time they were advanced, even revolutionary. And a good many of the principles enunciated in the latter part of the nineteenth century are as fresh and sound today as they were then.

Prisons, condemned as cesspools of degradation and breeding places of crime, gave way to reformatories. The theory was

[4] Cesare B. Beccaria, *An Essay on Crimes and Punishment* (London: printed for J. Alman, 1767), p. 165.
[5] *Ibid.*, p. 26.

that they would reeducate minds and redirect emotions, turning prisoners out reformed. The 1883 Conference referred to earlier was convened at the height of the reformatory movement, less than a decade after the establishment of pioneering Elmira Reformatory.

We have not yet fully realized the objectives set by those early reformers. Change has not been consistent. We have both some outmoded and some modern notions about crime and its treatment. We have a few relatively "good" correctional institutions, and many that destroy the spirit.

Probation and parole systems, too, run the gamut from reasonably efficient to "underfinanced moral gestures," as one was described in the 1930s. We shall gain nothing by denying we have yet a distance to go to translate into practice the ideals of the nineteenth-century social philosophers. But there has been progress, as we shall see throughout this volume.

2

ORIGINS OF PROBATION

Probation is a treatment program in which final action in an adjudicated offender's case is suspended, so that he remains at liberty, subject to conditions imposed by or for a court, under the supervision and guidance of a probation worker. The word "probation" derives from the Latin, its root meaning being "a period of proving or trial." The Catholic Church has used the term to connote a test period undergone by candidates seeking membership in religious orders. In Protestant denominations ministerial candidates may be "on probation" pending ordination.

In the correctional field, probation is a treatment program designed to facilitate the social readjustment of offenders. The program rests upon the court's power to suspend sentence. The probation period is served in the community rather than in a correctional institution. Suspension of final action is conditional, contingent upon the probationer's adherence to regulations set by the court or at the judge's behest. A probationer is supervised and counseled by an agent of the court. Should he seriously breach the conditions imposed, probation may be revoked, in which case the court will invoke the appropriate penalty.

The theory of probation evolved from antecedent practices, all intended to lessen or otherwise mitigate the severities of the penal code. In English common law the courts were presumed to have power to suspend sentence for specified purposes and periods. On this basic authority rest the devices which preceded probation.

Benefit of Clergy

Benefit of clergy is usually cited as a forerunner of probation, although this seems a bit far-fetched. It dates back to the thirteenth century, when many felonies were punishable by death, in English statutory law. The Church insisted that only ecclesiastical tribunals had jurisdiction over members of the clergy. Therefore, benefit of clergy was initiated as a device by which ordained clerks, monks, and nuns, accused of crime, could claim the benefit and have their cases transferred to Church courts. As monarchical power increased, Henry II insisted that an ordained individual who ran afoul of secular law should be tried in a secular court. As a compromise, however, such persons were permitted to claim benefit of clergy in the Crown's courts, and a real benefit it was. When a member of the cloth, suspected of crime, was brought into the King's Court, his bishop could claim the dispensation for him. Thereupon, the charge was read to the cleric, but no evidence was presented against him. Instead, he gave his own version of the alleged offense and brought in witnesses to corroborate his testimony. With all the evidence against the accused expunged and only favorable witnesses testifying, it is hardly astounding that most cases ended in acquittal. When, occasionally, a defendant was found guilty, he was "degraded" and "put to penance," but rarely was that penance a rope around the neck, as was often the outcome for defendants not entitled to benefit of clergy.

By the middle of the fourteenth century the benefit was extended to certain other categories of defendants, provided they could read. To prove their ability, they usually were given a passage from the Psalms: "Have mercy upon me, O God, according to thy lovingkindness: according unto the multitude

of thy tender mercies blot out my transgressions." Because
thereafter these transgressions were frequently adjudicated
leniently, the selection came to be known as the "neck verse,"
since so often it was used to escape the death penalty. Later,
the literacy test became a fiction. With the knowledge and approval of the judge, a clerk would report that a defendant could
read even when he could not, and the jurist allowed the benefit
if he saw fit.

As benefit of clergy, in time, was offered to more and more
classes of the accused, it lost its special, clerical meaning entirely and became "a clumsy set of rules which operated in
favour of all criminals to mitigate in certain cases the severity
of the criminal law." [1] But as the State gained ascendancy over
the Church, benefit of clergy fell into disuse. It was abolished
for commoners in 1827, and for peers in 1841. The American
colonies entertained the plea until shortly after the Revolution.

While benefit of clergy provided alleviation of sentence, it
offered none of the features pointed up in our definition of
probation.

Judicial Reprieve

More directly related to probation was judicial reprieve, a
temporary suspension of the imposition or execution of sentence. Its purpose was to allow a stay so the defendant might
apply to the Crown for an absolute or conditional pardon. The
defendant usually remained at liberty pending final disposition of his case.

We have here, then, suspension of sentence, but no conditions regarding behavior were imposed during such suspension.
And there was no supervision by an agent of the court.

[1] W. S. Holdsworth, *A History of English Law*, III, 294, quoted in *Probation
and Related Matters* (New York: United Nations, Department of Social
Affairs, 1951), footnote, p. 17.

Recognizance

Much closer to probation was recognizance, which comes
from the Latin *recognoscere,* meaning to "recall to mind." It
was, and is, a bond or obligation entered into by a defendant,
who thus binds himself to refrain from doing, or to do, something for a stipulated period, and to appear in court on a
specified date for trial or for final disposition of the case. Entering into a recognizance, also called "binding over," might or
might not require that the person post monetary bond as
surety. Should he fail to abide by the terms of the agreement,
the debt he owed the State would become enforceable, whether
that meant forfeiture of bond or incarceration or both.

By the nineteenth century, recognizance was being utilized
in dealing with young and petty offenders particularly, both
in England and New England. It was employed before trial
and as a conditional disposition upon conviction.

In this legal procedure we find some features common to
modern probation: suspension of sentence; freedom in lieu of
incarceration; conditions set upon such freedom; and the possibility of revocation of liberty upon violation of the conditions.
But recognizance provided no official supervision or guidance
by an officer of the court.

The earliest recorded use of recognizance in our country
was in the case of *Commonwealth* v. *Chase,* heard before
Judge Oxenbridge Thacher, of the Municipal Court of Boston,
in 1830. He set forth the nature of the practice in his statement:

The indictment against Jerusha Chase was found at the January
term of this court. . . . She pleaded guilty to the same, and sentence would have been pronounced at that time, but upon the
application of her friends, and with the consent of the attorney of
the commonwealth, she was permitted, upon her recognizance for
her appearance in this court whenever she should be called for, to
go at large. It has sometimes been practiced in this court, in cases

of peculiar interest, and in the hope that the party would avoid the commission of any offense afterwards, to discharge him on a recognizance of this description. The effect is that no sentence will ever be pronounced against him, if he shall behave himself well afterwards, and avoid any further violation of the law.[2]

Bail

A judge may direct release on recognizance with or without bail, or sureties. And bail is used with or without recognizance. Originally, it was a method of assuring a defendant's appearance for trial, and also of effecting provisional suspension of final action in a case. Today it is used exclusively for the first purpose.

Earlier, the defendant was placed in the custody of those who became bail for his appearance in court. The sureties who "went bail" therefore had a financial interest in seeing to it he abided by the court's instructions. This necessarily entailed some supervision, to make sure the accused did not decamp. Thus, in bail as a form of deferral of final action we had suspension of sentence, freedom instead of incarceration, conditions set upon that freedom, the possibility of its revocation, and some kind of supervision, although not by an official agent of the court.

The United Nations report, *Probation and Related Matters*, calls recognizance and provisional release on bail "in a very real sense the first, rudimentary stage in the development of probation."[3]

Filing of Cases

Filing of cases was a practice apparently peculiar to Massachusetts in the nineteenth century. The imposition of sentence was suspended when, upon a verdict of guilty in a

[2] Frank W. Grinnell, "Probation as an Orthodox Common Law Practice in Massachusetts Prior to the Statutory System," *Massachusetts Law Quarterly*, II (1916–17), 591–639.

[3] *Op. cit.*, p. 22.

criminal proceeding, the court recognized extenuating circumstances justifying mitigation of the penalty. The case was "filed." It might also be filed when a legal question in a similar case was awaiting action on appeal, and the higher court's decision would possibly establish a new interpretation binding upon like situations. When the judge, with consent of the defendant and prosecutor, filed the case, he made the defendant subject to conditions he set forth.

The filing of a case did not constitute final judgment. It left it within the province of the court to take further action at any time, upon motion of either defense or prosecution. Such action might be an order of imprisonment but, upon proof that the defendant had been comporting himself properly, the judge could continue the case on file indefinitely, the net result being that the individual was in effect a free man.

Probation

We come now to probation as we define it today. Historians usually call it an origination of the United States, John Augustus being named the "father" of probation. There is no doubt Augustus pioneered in probation. And he was certainly its local father as well as the first probation officer in the world. But something very like his work was born practically simultaneously in Great Britain. The coincidence need not surprise us. An innovation occurs when the time is right. Then it sometimes springs to life in different places simultaneously, because the requisite groundwork has been done. As Darwin was crystallizing his theories, scientists on the Continent were arriving at similar insights on the origin of species. The juvenile court became a reality in two states at almost the same time. Medical social work came into use in two hospitals, both in Boston, in the same year, one institution unaware of the development in the other.

The social climate was right for the birth of probation in the

nineteenth century. Thoughtful observers had become convinced that prisons were not "teaching a lesson," penitentiaries
were not making inmates penitent. It was also coming clear that
suspension of sentence without provision for supervision and
guidance of the released person served little purpose. So it was
that Matthew Davenport Hill, of Birmingham, England, pioneered in his country in 1841, the very year John Augustus performed a like service in Boston for the United States.

Hill was a young attorney in the 1820s when he observed an
experiment in Warwickshire Quarter Sessions. In selected cases
of youthful offenders, magistrates imposed token sentences of
one day, on condition the defendant remain under the care
of an approved parent or master thereafter. This was no suspension of sentence, but it did represent mitigation of punishment and supervision of the offender in the community. However, no conditions were laid down, nor was there provision for
revocation of freedom in the event the offender misbehaved.

Early in 1841, Hill, now Recorder, decided to institute a
modified version of this system in his court. Instead of requiring the day in jail, he suspended sentence and placed the
defendant under the supervision of a guardian. He saw his
program as rehabilitative, not punitive, justifying it on the
ground "there would be better hope of amendment under such
guardians than in the gaol of the county." [4] Thus, England had
a demonstration of a correctional program which, although not
called probation, had some of its elements as practiced by
Augustus in Boston. Hill selected appropriate cases, suspended
sentence, and provided for supervision. Unlike the Boston
court, Hill's court retained no legal control over the released
offender once he was turned over to his guardian. If the defendant misconducted himself, no sanctions were imposed.

---

[4] Matthew Davenport Hill, *Suggestions for the Repression of Crime,
Contained in Charges Delivered to Grand Juries of Birmingham; Supported
by Additional Facts and Arguments* (London, 1857), p. 117.

However, wrote Hill, should that individual commit another offense and come before him, he would take into consideration that he was dealing with a repeater. Hill dealt severely with such a defendant, "that the punishment should be such as to show that it was from no weakness, from no mistaken indulgence, from no want of resolution on the part of the court to perform its duty" that leniency had been extended before.[5]

Other jurists, impressed with Hill's experiment, began using recognizances, mainly with young first offenders. And Hill, seeking more certain protection for the community, asked the chief superintendent of police to make periodic inquiries into the conduct of persons released to guardians. These investigations were conducted by confidential officers who visited homes without prior notice.

In the United States, judges were also wrestling with the problem of humanizing justice. They were not wholly unprepared for a John Augustus, as we have already seen in the instance of Judge Thacher.

Augustus was a man of strong convictions, burning zeal, and limitless compassion. Born at Woburn, Massachusetts, in 1784, he was a cordwainer (bootmaker) at twenty-one, living in Lexington and carrying on his flourishing business from his home. In 1827 he moved to Boston, where he continued his occupation.

In 1841, at the age of fifty-seven, Augustus became interested in court work. He describes the eventful day in a little volume published some years later:

In the month of August, 1841, I was in court one morning, when the door communicating with the lockroom was opened and an officer entered, followed by a ragged and wretched looking man, who took his seat upon the bench allotted to prisoners. I imagined from the man's appearance, that his offence was that of yielding to his appetite for intoxicating drinks, and in a few moments I found

[5] *Ibid.*, p. 118.

that my suspicions were correct, for the clerk read the complaint, in which the man was charged with being a common drunkard. The case was clearly made out, but before sentence had been passed, I conversed with him for a few moments, and found that he was not yet past all hope of reformation. . . . He told me that if he could be saved from the House of Correction, he never again would taste intoxicating liquors; there was such an earnestness in that tone, and a look of firm resolve, that I determined to aid him; I bailed him, by permission of the Court. He was ordered to appear for sentence in three weeks from that time. He signed the pledge and became a sober man; at the expiration of this period of proba-tion, I accompanied him into the court room. . . . The Judge ex-pressed himself much pleased with the account we gave of the man, and instead of the usual penalty,—imprisonment in the House of Correction,—he fined him one *cent* and costs, amounting in all to $3,76, which was immediately paid. The man continued industrious and sober, and without doubt has been by this treatment, saved from a drunkard's grave.[6]

Note that the word *probation* is used in this passage. John Augustus was the first to employ it in the correctional frame of reference. In this selection from his writings we also find most of the features listed in our definition of probation. Augustus looked upon his work with offenders as treatment. In the light of modern knowledge we might smile at Augustus's belief he could discern from a man's demeanor and speech that he had a "firm resolve" to quit liquor and that he was "not yet past all hope of reformation." But Augustus must be judged in the context of the times. Psychology, psychiatry, social work, were in their infancy, although the great Dr. Benjamin Rush, "father of American psychiatry," had done his work, and Octavia Hill in England, and others in this country, were before much longer to fashion social work into a profession. Augustus was a product of his era, and ahead of it, too.

[6] John Augustus, *A Report of the Labors of John Augustus, for the Last Ten Years, in Aid of the Unfortunate* (Boston: Wright & Hasty, 1852); reprinted as *John Augustus, First Probation Officer* (New York: National Probation Association, 1939), pp. 4–5.

In the disposition of the case of the "common drunkard," who was probably unawed by the fact he was making history, we have the suspended sentence, accompanied by freedom in the community rather than incarceration, and conditions placed upon that freedom. We have supervision and counseling, but not by an official agent of the court. Had the probationer not behaved satisfactorily, his freedom would have been revoked and he would have begun to serve his sentence in the House of Correction. To be sure, we would not today believe that a three-week period of probation and sobriety proved much, but this, again, needs to be seen against the historical background.

Beginning with that one intemperate defendant, John Augustus devoted himself to probation work. He was convinced that many offenders required no more than the sincere interest of another human being to be able to straighten out their lives. Augustus housed some of his charges in the large house he occupied with his family; other probationers had homes to which they could return. John fed and clothed the needy, required those who should work to seek and keep at it. Eventually, he went bail for women too and then for youths. He interested himself in alcoholics, petty thieves, felons, prostitutes, but always with discrimination:

Great care was observed of course, to ascertain whether the prisoners were promising subjects for probation, and to this end it was necessary to take into consideration the previous character of the person, his age and the influences by which he would in future be likely to be surrounded.[7]

Time proved the Boston shoemaker a shrewd judge of character; for, according to his records, most of his probationers seem to have changed for the better.

So dedicated was Augustus to his probation work that his private business suffered. Hours he might have been working he spent in prowling the courts instead. Reported the *Rambler,* a local journal:

[7] *Ibid.,* p. 34.

In the Police Court, Mr. Augustus seems the most at home. As he
enters the room, he casts his eye towards the prisoners' bench, where
are seated perhaps, half a dozen miserable beings, bruised and
ragged, and trembling from the effects of a recent debauch. It is
probable that some of them know him, for as he walks to the box
two or three turn their blood-shot eyes toward him with eager
glances. . . . In a moment he is with them, gently reproving the
hardened ones, and cheering . . . those in whom are visible signs
of penitence.[8]

He was walking about in Leveret Street Jail one day, when
he saw a small boy, crying bitterly:

I asked him why he was there, and he said he did not know. I inquired of the officers and they informed me that he was there on
a charge of committing rape. . . . I afterwards learned, that such
was the fact. He was but *seven* years old. I proceeded directly to
court, and informed his Honor . . . of the fact. The judge immediately issued a *capias* and the child was brought into court. . . .
A jury was impaneled. . . . I told the judge that I thought it a
shame and a disgrace to all present to proceed with the case; his
Honor asked what could be done; I replied, "let him be sent to his
mother and placed in her lap"; I stated that I would bail him, and
to this the court readily assented.[9]

In another case, two boys playing together got into an im-
broglio. As boys will, one grabbed the other's cap and took off.
The aggrieved youngster pursued, seized the fleeing felon, and
forcibly extracted from his pocket the sum of six cents. The
two then separated, each no doubt running home to tell mother.
Then, as happens, one boy repented his sin and visited the
other, returning the purloined cap. That lad graciously accepted it, but when asked, as *quid pro quo*, to give back the six
pennies, saw no logic in this. One thing led to another; the
parents got into it, as parents will; and the penny-snatcher
wound up in police court and then in jail, charged with highway robbery.

If ever a case warranted probation, this was it. The lad's

<hr>

[8] *Ibid.*, p. 75.   [9] *Ibid.*, p. 95.

father begged Augustus to bail his son, which he did. The parents settled their differences and, Mr. Augustus dryly remarks, "here ended the great highway robbery case." One of the boys was nine, the other ten.[10]

"The object of the law," Augustus declared, "is to reform criminals, and to prevent crime and not to punish maliciously, or from a spirit of revenge." [11] He made that clear to judges, police, and the world at large, so much so, and so vehemently, that a writer once remarked Augustus had a tongue "which appears to be hung in the middle and oiled at each end." [12] Such a tongue was bound to make him enemies, and with right good humor Augustus published some of the things they said about him. One Mike Walsh had this comment in a newspaper in 1848:

There are a number of lazy hypocritical knaves . . . who, by dint of unblushing impudence and affected kind-heartedness not only make a fat living by their mouthing professions, but actually pass with the credulous . . . for real disinterested philanthropists . . .

. . . We have been partly led into these remarks by the conduct of a fellow who is called John Augustus . . .

Mr. Augustus seems to have a great itching for notoriety, and dollars; . . . he hangs and loafs about the Police and Municipal Courts, almost every day, and takes more airs upon himself than all the judges and officers . . .

. . . We know something about this Peter Funk philanthropist, and pea-nut reformer, and unless he conducts himself henceforth with a great deal more propriety, we shall take it upon ourself to teach him decency.[13]

It is of no little significance that much of the criticism then directed at probation is still heard. Summing up his work, Augustus wrote:

Those who are opposed to this method, tell us that it is rather an incentive to crime, and therefore, instead of proving salutary, it is detrimental to the interest of society, and so far from having a tend-

[10] *Ibid.,* p. 96.   [11] *Ibid.,* p. 23.   [12] *Ibid.,* p. xiv.   [13] *Ibid.,* pp. 78–79.

ency to reform the persons bailed, it rather presents inducements
for them to continue a career of crime; the law is robbed of its
terrors, and its punishments, and there is nothing therefore, to deter
them from repeating the offence with which they were previously
charged . . .

. . . if a person who has been bailed, or received the leniency
of the court, proves false to his promises of amendment, people are
ever ready to predict that all others will conduct in a similar manner.[14]

Augustus worked eighteen years, aided financially and otherwise by civic-minded citizens whom he interested in probation.
In all, he bailed almost two thousand individuals. Out of the
first 1,100 on whom he kept records only one forfeited bond.
If, he reflected, "only one-half of this number have become reformed, I have ample cause to be satisfied" [15]—as who would
not?

When John Augustus died, in 1859, his work was carried on
by others. It still lacked one feature which we consider essential
today. Neither Augustus nor those who immediately followed
were officials of the court. Consequently, they lacked the authority and support which official probation officers now have.

In 1869 Massachusetts passed a law providing for the appointment of an agent to the Board of State Charities, to investigate cases of children tried before the courts. He was to
attend trials and receive such children for placement as the
court directed. Within a few years, about one third of all young
boys and girls appearing in court were being accorded probation.

In 1878 probation was regulated by statute for the first time
when Massachusetts provided for the appointment of a paid
probation officer for Boston's courts of criminal jurisdiction.
Thus, the officer became an official agent of the court. The
drafters of the statute clearly viewed probation as treatment
when they inserted the provision that "such persons as may

[14] *Ibid.*, pp. 99–100.   [15] *Ibid.*, p. 96.

reasonably be expected to be reformed without punishment"
be selected for probation. It is interesting, too, that no restrictions on eligibility for probation were laid down. It was available to all offenders, juvenile and adult, male and female, felon
and misdemeanant, regardless of the particulars of the offense.

The enactment provided for the appointment by the Mayor
of Boston of a suitable person from the ranks of the police, or
from the citizenry at large, to act as probation officer. He was to
be under the "general control" of the police chief. His duties
included attending court, investigating prisoners charged with,
or convicted of, crime, and making recommendations to judges
on the advisability of placing defendants on probation. He was
to visit probationers, help encourage them, check on their activities, and make reports to the chief of police. He had the
power to rearrest a probationer, with the approval of the
police chief, after which the court would proceed to make such
disposition as was within the judge's power.

Lieutenant Henry C. Hemmenway was the first statutory
probation officer in the United States, although Captain E. H.
Savage is more commonly accorded that honor, probably because Hemmenway served but four months. Savage, a former
chief of police, succeeded him, remaining in his post fourteen
years, at a salary of $1,500 annually.

In 1880 authority to appoint probation officers was extended
to all cities and towns in Massachusetts. This was a permissive
bill only, and few jurisdictions took advantage of it.

In 1891 Massachusetts provided for statewide probation.
The courts, rather than municipal authorities, were to appoint
probation officers. It was stipulated that "they shall not be
active members of the regular police force," this apparently
having appeared a hazard. An officer was to be appointed in
each police district and municipal court. In 1898 the probation
system was extended to superior courts.

Probation got off to a slow start elsewhere. Missouri enacted a law in 1897, Vermont a year later. (Incidentally, in the latter state the bill was titled, "An Act relating to the parole of prisoners," indicating that the terms "probation" and "parole" were used interchangeably and creating a confusion not yet dissipated.) Illinois, Minnesota, and Rhode Island entered the ranks in 1899; New Jersey, in 1900.

There were intriguing variations in these early statutes. Illinois and Minnesota provided for juvenile probation only. Rhode Island, the first to place restrictions on eligibility, excluded from probation those convicted of certain offenses. Vermont initiated the county plan of organization, each such unit appointing its officers and administrators, and operating autonomously, within the framework of the state's enabling act. In contradistinction, Rhode Island pioneered a statewide, state-controlled administration.

It was the juvenile court movement which accelerated the development of probation, for the latter was an integral part of the program of these special courts. In 1899 Illinois established a juvenile court in Chicago. Probation officers were appointed by, and responsible to, the judge. They were not paid out of public funds, partly due to the dubious assumption that to offer salaries would attract individuals interested only in the compensation. Volunteers, it was felt, would be men and women of great heart, working for the sheer joy of serving mankind.

As the juvenile court movement progressed, so did legislation authorizing probation for juveniles. But not until 1945 was the roster of states complete.[16]

Adult probation grew more slowly. By 1910, only twenty-one states and the District of Columbia had enabling statutes. In 1930 the count stood at thirty states plus the Federal criminal courts system. By 1950, legislation permitting adult probation existed in forty-four states. The exceptions were Mississippi, Nevada, New Mexico, and South Dakota.

[16] The last holdout was Wyoming.

Nevada got a law through in 1951. Two years later, New Mexico drafted permissive legislation for an adult probation system, leaving it to judges to decide whether they wished to implement the law in their respective jurisdictions. South Dakota entered the ranks in 1955; Mississippi, one year later.

It took a long time, but we now have legislation in each state authorizing both juvenile and adult probation in at least certain courts. Most states make their probation acts applicable to all benches, but some except those handling misdemeanants.

One issue remained to be settled. It will be recalled that probation and its forerunners were based on the common law conception that judges had authority to suspend sentences. The common law is "found," not written. It is custom as defined in judicial opinions on specific cases. Common law gave England and the United States power to suspend either the imposition or the execution of sentence on a temporary basis and for specified purposes, as in recognizance. The question remained whether a court was empowered to suspend a sentence for an indefinite period, meaning as a disposition and not merely as a stay for such specified purposes. English jurists assumed they lacked the inherent power to do this, but legal opinion in the United States was split.

The United States case most often cited as authority for indefinite suspension was *People* ex rel. *Forsyth* v. *Court of Sessions*.[17] The court had before it a young man known to be of good character and reputation prior to the offense. There were mitigating circumstances surrounding the commission of the crime, in the judge's opinion. He suspended imposition of sentence during good behavior.

The district attorney contended that the right to suspend indefinitely did not exist in common law and that the court must impose sentence, since no procedural stay was intended, to allow appeal or other action. The New York statute authorizing suspension of sentence was invalid, he declared, and an

[17] 141 N.Y. 288, 36 N.E. 386 (1894).

infringement on the executive power of pardon. This was an
important legal contention; for probation, which rests upon the
power to suspend sentence, was now in use in various parts of
the country and a decision striking down suspension would
cripple the service.

The New York Court of Appeals considered the case and
upheld the trial court and the constitutionality of the statute
involved. But the issue would not die. Courts in other states
were using indefinite suspension, and finally a challenge of
such practice reached the United States Supreme Court, in
1916.

The case involved originated in the Federal court system. In
1915 United States Attorney General T. W. Gregory had been
agitating against indefinite suspension. His views were expressed by Assistant Attorney General William Wallace, Jr.:

Let the judges confine themselves to their true function of admin-
istering rather than thwarting the law; . . . if the guilt is established, let the judge impose the punishment decreed by law . . . so
that the court when so acting may be enforcing the law and not
flying into the very teeth of it.[18]

Gregory found the test case he wanted in the Northern District of Ohio. Judge John M. Killits had suspended the execution of a five-year sentence of a young man who pleaded guilty
to making false entries and embezzling money from the bank
where he was employed. He had no prior record, made full
restitution, and the bank's officers did not wish to prosecute.

Gregory came into Killits's court and moved the jurist's
order be vacated, the Attorney General arguing that the court
had exceeded its authority. Killits overruled the motion, and
the issue was joined.

The United States Supreme Court handed down a unanimous
decision on December 4, 1916, delivered by Chief Justice Ed-

[18] Charles Lionel Chute and Marjorie Bell, *Crime, Courts, and Probation*
(New York: Macmillan, 1956), p. 94.

ward D. White.[19] It held that Federal courts (and, inferentially, state benches as well) lacked inherent power to
suspend sentences permanently or indefinitely. There was, the
court averred, no right "to continue a practice which is incon-
sistent with the Constitution." The decision did not invalidate
recognizance, but held only that while "common law courts
possessed the power by recognizances to secure good behavior,
that is to enforce the law," this did not support "the proposition that those courts possessed the arbitrary discretion to
permanently decline to enforce the law." The Court was saying,
in other words, that indefinite suspensions were without legal
sanction.

Instead of crippling probation, the decision in the Killits
case actually helped it. The explosion of the doctrine of inherent power to suspend indefinitely meant, to many judges
and others interested in the subject, only that laws must be
written that specifically conferred upon courts by statute what
the common law had not given them. This was done, and there
is now no question that courts do have the power to suspend
sentences for indefinite periods when placing defendants on
probation.

CHARLES LIONEL CHUTE

The history of probation would be incomplete without a
word about Charles Lionel Chute. If John Augustus fathered
American probation, Charles Chute helped it grow up.

Charlie, as he was affectionately known, helped found the
National Probation Association (NPA) and became its executive director in 1921. He served in that capacity until his retirement in 1948.

As head of the organization (later called the National Probation and Parole Association), he carried on a determined educational campaign, showed himself a master organizer, pro-

[19] *Ex parte United States*, 242 U.S. 27–53 (1916).

moter, and public relations man. The NPA made countless
surveys pointing up the need for probation services in a number of areas. It fought for the extension of the juvenile court. It
organized conventions where correctional workers could exchange views. Chute battled for a merit system in probation.
He convinced hostile and indifferent judges that they should
make full use of probation in their courts.

An example of his patience and skill in human relations was
his tireless fight for a probation system in the Federal courts.
He began his campaign in 1916, against the open and vociferous
opposition of members of that bench.[20] One judge wrote him:

> I most sincerely hope that you will fail in your efforts . . .
> . . . in England and in Canada a man is either at liberty after
> a trial and acquittal, or with a discolored ring around his neck dead
> within thirty days after he has sent some one into eternity . . .
> . . . In this country, due to the efforts of people like yourselves,
> the murderer has a cell bedecked with flowers and is surrounded
> by a lot of silly people.[21]

Chute preferred to move forward by common consent, but if
he could not go ahead on a matter of principle, he dug in and
stubbornly stood his ground, snipers be damned. In this matter
he outwaited his critics, treated them with such candor and
respect that many were won over. He outmaneuvered Attorney
General Harry M. Daugherty, whose assistant wrote that the
drive for a probation system was "all a part of a wave of
maudlin rot of misplaced sympathy for criminals." [22] Chute
and friends of the NPA sought out congressmen and senators,
including those who opposed probation because they favored
prohibition and feared the former would make it easier for
violators of the Volstead Act to escape dire punishment. On

---

[20] For this description of the battle for a Federal probation system I have
relied on Chute and Bell, *op. cit.*, pp. 89–111, as well as on many personal con-
versations with Chute.

[21] *Ibid.*, p. 106.   [22] *Ibid.*, p. 107.

one Washington trip, Chute's forces buttonholed all the House leaders, the General Counsel of the Anti-Saloon League, Assistant Attorney General William J. Donovan, Secretary of the Navy Curtis D. Wilbur, and President Coolidge himself. Mr. Chute's report to his NPA committee read: "We feel that much of the opposition of the drys has been removed. . . . Ninety-six members of the House have pledged their support . . . We are carrying on a campaign to reach every member." [23]

On March 4, 1925, the President approved a bill placing the first Federal probation law on the books.

He was a short man, this dynamic Mr. Chute, with a shock of stiff, iron-gray hair and a habit of speaking out of the side of his mouth. Persons unaware of his history, observing his rumpled suit and ear-to-ear grin, sometimes treated him with condescension, as they might a genial, naïve farmer in town to see the sights. But, working with him, feeling the impact of his steel-trap mind, his genuine warmth and interest in people, these same individuals came to love and admire him.

Shortly before he retired, Charlie was saddened by the fact that several leaders in the field, who had started when he did, had lost their zeal for innovation and were defending the *status quo* as if it were gospel. It did not occur to him that they were older than they had been in 1913 or 1914. The reason it did not occur to him was because *he* had not grown old. He never lost his youthful spirit.

Before he died in 1953, he had coordinated the field, given it direction and momentum. Above all, he made it conscious of itself *as* a field and a profession. Many workers in corrections have contributed to the thinking in that field, but Charlie Chute, probably more than any one man in our time, gave it its rationale.

[23] *Ibid.,* p. 110.

THE RATIONALE OF PROBATION

That rationale begins with the assumption that certain offenders are reasonably safe risks in society by the time they appear in court; it would not facilitate their adjustment to remove them to institutions, and the move might well have the opposite effect. Meantime, the community would provide for their dependents. And the effect of such incarceration upon the prisoner's family would be incalculable. If, then, the community would not be jeopardized by a defendant's presence, and if he gave evidence of ability to change to a law-abiding life, it served both society and the individual to give him that chance, conditionally, under supervision and guidance.

AIMS OF PROBATION

What are the aims of modern probation?

It seeks to help offenders, juvenile and adult, through services designed for the purpose, to solve those difficulties, personal and environmental, which brought them into conflict with law. The objective is "that these individuals become more comfortable in, part of, and identified with, social living in their communities." [24] At the same time, since stability is not achieved overnight, the probation service protects the community against the probationer who shows signs of recidivating.

[24] David Dressler, *Probation and Parole.* (New York: Columbia University Press, 1951), p. 4.

3

PROBATION TODAY

May armed robbers gain probation? Do probationers report in person? What determines the length of the probation period? Inquirers usually want unequivocal answers when they ask about probation practices. It is impossible to furnish them, for each state has its own basic probation law. And there are 3,068 counties, the majority of which operate autonomously within the framework of the applicable state statutes.[1] Practically nothing can be said that will apply to every jurisdiction. But some patterns do exist, some generalizations are valid, provided the reader constantly bears in mind that for every statement there probably is at least one exception.

Unit of Organization

The most prevalent form of organization is the county plan, in which the state writes basic probation law while each county, within that framework, appoints staff and administers its own department.

Centralized state probation systems are in the minority, but increasing in number. Here, one agency administers the system for the entire state, furnishing counties with requisite service.

There has been some trend toward the combined state-administered probation and parole agency. One organization

---

[1] Alaska and Hawaii have now been voted statehood by the Congress. However, so little information is available on probation and parole there that I have not included them in this rundown of practice.

furnishes both probation and parole services to the entire state.

There are city and town probation units, independent of the counties in which they are located. The city of New York, for instance, has a probation unit attached to certain of its municipal courts while county departments exist in other courts in the metropolitan area.

The Federal Government conducts its own probation program for persons coming under the purview of courts at that level.

Advocates of the county plan say the centralized state system impairs local autonomy. It does, to an extent. However, a state unit has much to recommend it. Many counties cannot afford adequate probation service. Under a state administration they would receive what they need, on a par with the rest of the state.

There is another argument for a centralized system. It may be illustrated by the hypothetical Smith family:

Jack Smith lives in that part of New York City which is called Manhattan. Manhattan is New York County, the boundaries of both being identical. Jack is on probation for burglary in the Court of General Sessions, New York County.

His brother Harry crosses the bridge into Brooklyn, which is Kings County, but also part of New York City. He steals a car, is on probation in Kings County.

Sister Mary does some shoplifting in the Bronx, is on probation to that county.

Brother Ralph, joy riding in Queens County, gets into a gang fight resulting in his placement on probation in Queens.

Finally, this being one of "those" families, Zelpha, who is married and living on Staten Island, slices her husband up a bit, is placed on probation to the Richmond County Court. She returns to the parental home pending a divorce.

The Smith family, then, resides in New York County. But four of its five members on probation are under the jurisdiction of other counties. Five different officers crisscross each

other's trails, visiting the Smith home. They submit five sep-
arate expense accounts, keep five sets of records, in five office
buildings. And five Smiths live in one domicile but travel to
five different reporting stations.

A centralized state organization yields uniform standards
of recruitment and operation; a minimum of duplicating services; economy of time and money.

Applicability

Probation is available to juveniles and adults, males and
females, felons and misdemeanants. Least developed are facilities for misdemeanants. This should concern us, for these
offenders require as much attention as do felons. True, some
are accidental violators of law who need little if any help
from probation and represent practically no risk in the community. But among misdemeanants are also to be found the
alcoholics, the drug addicts, the petty thieves, vagrants, and
certain types of sex offender. All of these tend to be more dis-
organized personally, less capable of solving their problems,
than are felons. And in individual instances they may be more
dangerous than the latter. Yet the public considers misdemeanants lesser offenders. "After all," we say, "they're not
serious criminals, like robbers." The result is that government
does not spend much on probation service for these "lesser
offenders." Caseloads are fantastically high. Presentence investigations, if made at all, are necessarily superficial.

Consider the case of Albert Howard Fish: [2]

In 1929, Fish was in court on a relatively minor offense—passing
a worthless check. He received a misdemeanor sentence, suspended,
and was on probation for 90 days.

No presentence investigation had been prepared, for the heavily

[2] For this case history I have consulted Frederic Wertham, *The Show of
Violence* (New York: Doubleday & Co., 1949). Additionally, I have used
personal recollections, based upon my contact with Fish in my official
capacity.

loaded court could not afford one. Had there been such investigation, the judge would have been put on notice that the mild-looking
defendant was fantastically dangerous.

Here is what an investigation *could* have disclosed:

In two generations, seven members of the Fish family had mental
breakdowns or exhibited most eccentric behavior. Albert finished
elementary school at 15, worked regularly thereafter. On the surface he was a normal, healthy individual, although even then in-
choately drawn to fantasying curious sexual behavior. But such im-
aginings had little effect upon his outward conduct, and at 28 he
married. He sired six children, of whom he was exceedingly fond.

He had been wed 20 years when his wife eloped with another
man. Fish continued to take care of his offspring, but his behavior
gradually became eccentric. There were increasing periods of unemployment. He contracted three "marriages," all illegal since he
never divorced his vanished wife. He began to neglect his children.
And somewhere along the line he took to enacting those scenes he
had only imagined in childhood. He embraced practically every form
of extreme sexual perversion known to the medical profession.

Had there been an investigation in that court, in 1929, the probation officer almost certainly would have learned, from Fish himself,
some of the macabre, horrible details, for the voluble defendant
loved to talk about them. Over the years he had indulged in no
fewer than eighteen kinds of sexual deviation, particularly of the
sado-masochistic variety. He enjoyed torturing himself, and on a
number of occasions stuck needles into his spine and under his toe-
nails. He lured little boys and girls with candy, took them captive,
tortured them for days. He wrote obscene letters to women who
advertised in matrimonial journals. He was a fetishist, sodomist,
necrophiliac, and, withal, a religious hysteric. Sometimes he fancied
himself God; at other times, he punished himself for sinning against
God.

All these facts, remember, were in Fish's background when he
appeared in court on the check charge. And some were on record,
awaiting evaluation. But there was no time for evaluation. The
defendant had a history of eight prior arrests. He had been on
probation and on parole. The colorless listing of his criminal record
meant little, in the absence of fill-in. There had been some stealing,
uttering of worthless checks—the work of a "lesser offender." One

entry should have been a cue to something else: Fish served a misdemeanor term for sending obscene letters through the mails.

The record also revealed two periods of observation in psychiatric hospitals, but since he was not found psychotic on either occasion, the court hearing Fish's case in 1929 could not afford the luxury of pursuing the matter.

In short, because misdemeanants are the forgotten men and women of probation, the judge was not aware that Albert Fish had committed aberrant acts in twenty-three states over several decades. Most important, the court did not know that Fish stood before the bench with his hands figuratively dripping with blood. He was a killer at the time he answered the charge of writing a worthless check. He had kidnapped innumerable children, subjected them to unspeakable abuse, slaughtered somewhere between eight and fifteen of them.

One of his victims was Grace, age 10. Fish choked her to death, hacked off her head with a cleaver, then sawed her body in two. He placed some of the flesh in a kettle, seasoned it with onion, carrots, and bacon. For nine days he ate the human stew, in a state of hysterical sexual excitement.

The court, not being privy to these horrendous facts, treated Fish as a check passer. He finished probation "satisfactorily," since there was insufficient field service to permit discovery of his aberrant acts even then. This is indeed an indictment of society for its niggardly financing of probation in the misdemeanor court. Certainly it would not have taken much beyond a halfway workable caseload to permit revelation of what Fish was. But he finished probation and continued his bloody career.

Like some others of similar propensities, Fish had a compulsion to destroy himself by confession. In 1934, he wrote Grace's mother, practically tracing out a path to his door. Police followed his clues and walked in on him. He greeted them amiably, and eagerly relived his experiences in a confession.

Given adequate probation service somewhere along the way, Albert Fish would have been recognized for the dangerous man he was. He might have been hospitalized before he killed.

Men of his sort go in and out of misdemeanor courts. They

will continue to do so unless we protect ourselves by more
generous budgeting of probation departments of misdemeanor
courts.

Court Appearance

The adult offender appears in a court of criminal jurisdiction. If guilt has been ascertained, a presentence investigation
is initiated in courts providing such service. On the strength
of this, the judge may order the defendant imprisoned or may
place him on probation.

The juvenile is petitioned into court. Proceedings are informal. In many jurisdictions the investigation is prepared
prior to the hearing. In such instances, it is not a presentence
but a prehearing probation report.

While we have defined probation in such manner as to indicate that the probationer has been convicted of crime or
adjudicated into the status of juvenile delinquent, it is possible, in a limited number of jurisdictions, for an individual to
be on probation without such conviction or adjudication. To
cite one instance, Massachusetts sometimes places complaints
on file, thus eschewing trial and conviction where this seems
in the public interest. In certain Federal district courts, youthful offenders are treated in similar fashion. In given cases, the
alleged offender being willing, he waives trial and agrees to
place himself under voluntary probation.

The objective is to spare the offender the stigma and other
consequences of conviction. But the practice involves some
hazard. Suppose the offender violates probation. Trying him
at that point might be difficult or impossible. Witnesses might
be unavailable. If available, their recollection of events might
no longer be accurate. However, so few cases are involved,
percentage-wise, that no serious problems seem to have developed through this informal use of probation.

Investigation

Judges seem to have recognized that the probation investigation is an invaluable prognostic guide. But some still insist, "I don't need a report to tell *me* whether a defendant belongs in prison or on probation. I look at him, the way he stands before me, and . . ." Laws intended to impress upon the judiciary the value of the reports have long been on the books. To be sure, a judge who is required to have a presentence or prehearing report before him may not read it, or, if he does, may pay it little respect; but the statutes obviously intend to have him expose himself to it.

These laws fall into three categories: (1) the judge may decide whether and when he wants a report; (2) reports must be prepared prior to sentence if probation is being considered; (3) investigations are to be made and reports submitted before sentence whether or not probation is under consideration. There are variations on these patterns, as where reports are mandatory in felony but not misdemeanor cases.

By law, or reasonable implication, every juvenile court is required to have an investigation report before it at some point. Only a minority of states require a presentence investigation in all adult cases, whether or not probation is contemplated.

Eligibility

It is the court which has legal authority to grant probation, although the judge may act on recommendation of the probation department.

If we believe in individualizing offenders, then the judge should have unrestricted authority to select for probation. However, legislatures and the public have been chary of allowing such carte blanche. This is partly a result of our dread of the offender, partly an indication that we do not have complete confidence in the judiciary. We think Judge A. might

be politically influenced or Judge Z. lack discernment. We
set up intended safeguards against unwise decisions.

Restrictions of some sort are placed upon the majority of
courts in the matter of eligibility for probation. Juvenile courts
are scarcely affected. In adult jurisdictions, statutory limitations fall into two broad categories: (1) those forbidding probation for defendants charged with designated offenses; and
(2) those excluding persons convicted of felony more than
once. Only seven states have no restrictions whatever.[3] In fourteen, the sole limitation is that those convicted of crimes punishable by death or by life imprisonment are ineligible. Since
for the most part (but not exclusively) this means prisoners
who have committed murder, the disqualification is of slight
importance numerically.

Among states disqualifying on the basis of offense there is
no uniformity. Theoretically, each law seeks to make ineligible
those defendants guilty of the most serious crimes. But what
is a serious crime? Ten states specify arson and rape. But
Michigan, while not disbarring such cases, does exclude armed
robbers and night burglars.

As to repeated convictions, ten states forbid probation for
individuals convicted of two or more felonies; two, if there
has been a prior term of imprisonment of whatever nature;
and two states exclude those convicted three times, whether
for felony or misdemeanor.

In Tennessee it is illegal to grant probation to a defendant
convicted of a crime punishable by a sentence of more than
five years. Alabama obviously takes a different position on
what constitutes serious crime, for it excludes those punishable by terms of more than ten years. In Louisiana the jury
must recommend probation before it can be extended in a
jury case.

[3] Maryland, New Hampshire, New Jersey, Oregon, Utah, Vermont, and
Wisconsin.

In the United Kingdom no restrictions whatever are placed on eligibility, so far as criminal record is concerned, yet to the best of our knowledge the recidivism rate is not higher among British probationers than among those in the United States. The Standard Probation and Parole Act, developed by correctional workers under the sponsorship of the National Probation and Parole Association, recommends there be no limitation or restriction whatever on selection for probation in the United States.

Who Sets Probation Conditions?

As it is the court which has the authority to select for probation, so it is also the bench which establishes the conditions. The judge has broad powers in this matter, with few restrictions.

The Probation Term

By what laws and rules must a judge be guided in setting a probation sentence?

Widest lattitude exists in juvenile cases, where the court generally may impose whatever period he sees fit, provided it does not exceed a stipulated maximum. The latter is based, not upon the particulars of the offense, but on the upper juvenile age limit. Probation practically always must terminate no later than the time the juvenile reaches majority.

Laws vary widely where adults are concerned. The term must not exceed the maximum period of commitment which could have been meted out for the offense, unless—rarely— the statute specifically authorizes such extension. Within this framework, the length of the probation period is discretionary with the judge in most jurisdictions. However, in some states it may not exceed a stipulated period of time. For example, in Mississippi first offenders may be placed on probation for a term not to exceed five years. In other states, the stipulated

maximum varies by offense, type of court, or other factor. A
robbery conviction might carry a maximum probation term
of five years; a burglary count, three. A defendant in a court
of felony jurisdiction might be subject to a five-year maximum;
one in a lower court, to two years.

In a few states restrictions have to do with minima rather
than maxima. A New Jersey probationer must remain under
supervision at least a year. In Idaho, Montana, and Wisconsin,
felony offenders on probation are required to remain in that
status at least as long as the minimum term of imprisonment
to which they were subject.

Once more it must be remarked that if we are to individualize offenders, restrictions on probation term should be at the
irreducible minimum and related to treatment needs and community protection rather than to preconceived legal formulae.

Supervision

The time a probationer spends under care is called the
"supervision period," a somewhat unfortunate designation,
since it places all the emphasis upon the directive and pro-
tective function while seemingly ignoring the equally important treatment role. Actually, the probationer is under supervision *and* treatment. Community protection and individual
guidance go hand in hand.

Supervision, to use the conventional term, runs the gamut
in quality from routine acceptance of mailed reports to exercise
of the most advanced techniques in social work.

Violation of Probation

When may probation be revoked?

Every probation statute, by express language or reasonable
implication, provides that probation may be revoked for any
violation of conditions. Probation, like parole, is a privilege,
not a right. The probationer has been permitted to remain at

large by grace of the court. The judge sets conditions upon that freedom. He has the power to order revocation.

Whether stipulated in law or not, most courts give probationers cited for violation an opportunity to be heard before action is taken.

Revocation may result from: (1) general misconduct, that is, violation of the rules and regulations imposed; (2) absconding; (3) commission of a new offense.

Discharge

The court is the authority for discharging a probationer from supervision. Such termination occurs when the probation period has been satisfactorily completed. The effect of discharge is to relieve erstwhile probationers of responsibility to the court.

Status of Probation

Not many years ago, the correctional worker who suggested that probation (or parole) was less than perfect in operation was regarded by many of his colleagues as subversive. Today, honest criticism is more acceptable. Certainly it is essential to progress.

Workers now engage in considerable self-evaluation. They are more ready to acknowledge that a wide gap exists between theory and practice, the ideal and the real. They point to the need for better recruitment techniques, higher standards of administration, more effective treatment.

Speaking for the judiciary, in the official organ of the National Probation and Parole Association, Bolitha J. Laws, Chief Judge of the United States District Court, Washington, D.C., states:

Less than one-third of the nation's criminal courts have probation service which can be considered adequate. In a little more than one-

third, what exists is, at best, a token service; the remainder have no
probation service at all.[4]

It is encouraging, however, that young people are pouring
into the field, scrutinizing it objectively, telling the world what
they see. The newcomer feels no need to defend older ways.
A consequence has been a greater acceptance of the need for
research. In the past we heard sincere officers declare that
"religion is the greatest aid to rehabilitation"; or, "comic books
make juvenile delinquents"; or, "punish the parent and the
child will behave." How did they know? By hunch and by hope.
We heard about Johnny, a bad, bad boy, destined for reform
school. The officer "established rapport," and "gave him six
months of casework, and today that boy is fine," etc. Few inquired how one "gives" casework. No one asked for the speakers' definitions of casework—and they were awesome and won-
drous at times. No one demanded proof that casework treatment was effective.

Today, practitioners want to know. They make objective
investigations, seek answers to their questions, and are not
afraid of those answers. Research is accumulating in professional journals, replacing acceptance on faith. We search out
etiological factors in delinquency and crime. We study the
dynamics of recidivism. We study biology, chemistry, psychology, medicine, social work, and other fields for what is
new and potentially useful to correctional practice.

How Probation Might Work

Let us follow a fictional Sam Jones through the probation
process:

Sam is an adult, convicted of robbery, which is a felony in
his state. The judge defers sentence pending receipt of a probation report.

---

[4] Bolitha J. Laws, "Criminal Courts and Adult Probation," *National Probation
and Parole Journal*, III (1957), 357.

The probation officer interviews Sam in jail, goes into the field, prepares his report.

Jones appears for sentence. The judge gives him a five-to-ten-year term and suspends its execution, placing the defendant on probation for three years. (He could have made it two, or six; we are merely citing one possibility.)

Sam has his initial interview with Mr. Barton, who will supervise him during his probation period. Barton explains what probation is, what it expects of Sam, and what help he can get from it in solving certain of his problems. The probation officer says he is here to help when he can, but it is also his duty to keep informed concerning the probationer's activities. Should there be serious violation of probation, Barton is obligated to report it to the judge.

The rules and regulations are discussed and explained. Sam is told he may expect supervisory visits to home and job. He must report to the officer every week. Eventually, if his behavior warrants, he will report less frequently.

Supervision begins. The chances are, if he has had prior contact with courts and the law, that Sam is somewhat afraid of the officer, suspicious of him. Barton will have to establish rapport with the probationer before Sam quits being evasive on certain subjects. Sam may tell Barton the truth about his earnings, or even why he lost his job, but he will not be so ready to admit where he was last night, nor will he volunteer that he punched his wife in the jaw.

Some of these facts Barton will dig out for himself. This is one reason he goes into the field. But if he is successful in getting Jones to believe the officer wants to help, not harm, him, it will become less necessary to pick up such data by leg work. The probationer will talk more frankly, will want to discuss problems. Barton will become more the guidance worker than the law enforcement officer. He will help Sam find a new job and straighten out his marital affairs.

Now Sam has been under supervision for two years and eleven months. He is one month short of finishing probation. Barton has not been entirely satisfied with Jones's conduct. He works regularly and his domestic life runs smoothly, but Sam does more drinking than he should, and, more disturbing, he still is evasive on this subject. Moreover, as Jones nears the end of his probation period, the officer becomes suspicious that Sam may have had something to do with a crime committed recently.

The suspicion once aroused, Barton has no alternative. He must investigate and either clear the probationer or cite him as a violator. He will notify the police if he finds Sam involved in crime.

Barton makes a thorough field check. He concludes that the probationer is innocent of crime. But he has been associating with one of the men who did commit the offense, and such association may in itself be considered a violation. Moreover, it could mean that while Jones is innocent of crime up to now, he is on the way to committing one.

Barton prepares a violation of probation report. He brings Sam before the judge. The latter decides he will not revoke probation, but, instead of allowing the probation to terminate a month hence, as it is due to do, he lengthens the term by an additional three years. Thus, Sam will have been on probation six years of his five-to-ten-year sentence if he finishes the period satisfactorily.

This time he makes it. He comes before the court, is discharged from probation. He has no further obligation to the court. The suspended sentence cannot be invoked against Jones in the future, even if he commits another crime.

But let us consider other alternatives. Assume the same original circumstances. Sam is on probation a year when the supervising officer develops suspicions. Investigation discloses Jones's drinking has become such a problem that his reversion to crime is likely. Sam is associating with a bad crowd, keeping late hours, frequenting questionable resorts, and failing to support his dependents. Barton submits a violation report charging misbehavior short of crime. The judge gives Sam an opportunity to hear the charges and answer to them. Sam's explanations do not satisfy His Honor. He orders probation revoked and the suspended sentence executed. Sam goes to prison.

Sam has been on probation a year. How long will his prison sentence be? Five to ten years. That is what it was when it was suspended and that is what it is now. It was held in abeyance. Now it is invoked.

Suppose Sam is on probation for one year, then absconds. The officer submits a report so charging. A warrant for Jones's arrest is issued.

Jones remains a fugitive for twelve years and is then apprehended. He had been under supervision for one year prior to absconding. Twelve more years have elapsed, a total of thirteen since his placement on probation. The suspended sentence was for five to ten years. Had Sam remained in good standing he would be through with probation by now. Had he served in prison his maximum sentence would have expired. Nevertheless, his probation time stopped running when he ceased reporting. Whenever apprehended, he would still "owe" the five to ten years, for he would not have finished probation. The judge can now order Jones to begin serving his sentence.

However, suppose in the years Jones has been missing he was a devoted family man, working regularly, getting into no trouble. (These facts would have been ascertained by the officer, who submits a supplementary violation report covering the years between the original absconding and apprehension of the probation violator.) The judge might feel that little good would result from imprisoning the probationer. In that case, he cancels the delinquency, and Sam is in good standing again. This might mean he is discharged from supervision. Or it might lead to another period of supervision.

Sam did not abscond; was not sent to prison for other misconduct; but two years after coming under supervision he is convicted of another felony. He is declared a violator; probation is revoked; the suspended sentence is ordered executed.

This could mean that Sam Jones must serve five to ten years before beginning his new sentence which is, let us say, ten to twenty years. In that case, he will serve the minimum of the first sentence before becoming eligible to be paroled to start service of the second.

But in many states the judge has discretionary power to permit such a prisoner to serve the two terms concurrently rather than consecutively. The first, and shorter, sentence thus fits into the longer one, so to speak. When Jones has served the minimum of the second he is eligible for parole, since the minimum of the first was completed before he became eligible on the longer sentence.

There is still another possibility, in some states. The judge can rule that the books are closed on the first offense. He will not penalize Jones for violating probation. Instead, he allows him to begin doing the second sentence, owing nothing further on the first.

So much for Sam Jones. Now, here is Bob Curry, 14, a juvenile, on probation. The judge told him he would be discharged in three years if all goes well.

The supervision process is much the same as in the case of Jones. There may be some differences in the officer-probationer relationship. Juveniles often relate positively and quickly to their probation officers.

Another difference is that the juvenile is more likely to re-

cidivate than the adult. He is more immature, uses poor judgment, cannot as readily foresee the consequences of his acts.

However, Bob Curry makes a fine adjustment, at school and
home. He and his probation officer get along well. Instead of
waiting for three years to elapse, the officer recommends that
probation be terminated at the expiration of a year. The judge,
having authority to shorten or lengthen a probation term, con-
curs. Bob is discharged.

Suppose Bob is on probation the full three years, with only
fair conduct. The judge may extend the supervision period, so
long as it does not run beyond the young man's minority.

Bob begins probation, but in short order reverts to his former
activities. He is brought before the judge, who revokes the
probation and sends him to a correctional institution.

Bob, on probation, absconds. He is apprehended while still
a juvenile. The judge could cancel the delinquency and rein-
state him on probation. He could order the boy into an institution. But if Bob is apprehended after reaching his majority, it is unlikely the court will chance a test by reassuming
jurisdiction. Rather, it will cancel delinquency and close the
case.

Assume Bob finishes his probation term and years later, as
an adult, is convicted of a felony. His juvenile delinquency
record does not make him a second offender. Should he be
convicted in a state which limits probation to first offenders,
Curry would be eligible.

4

ORIGINS OF PAROLE

Parole is a treatment program in which an offender, after serving part of a term in a correctional institution, is conditionally released under supervision and treatment by a parole worker.

The word "parole" stems from the French, meaning "promise." A dictionary definition is "word of honor." Probably the term was first used in a correctional context in 1847, by Samuel G. Howe, the Boston penal reformer.

Like probation, parole is a treatment program, in the interest of society and individual. But the parolee, unlike the probationer, has served part of a term in a correctional institution. His release is conditional, contingent upon satisfactory behavior. He is under supervision and treatment by a person trained in parole work.

European Origins

England's contribution to what later metamorphosed into parole was its program of transportation to the American colonies, a program motivated, not by humanitarian considerations, but by economic pressures.

In the sixteenth century, England's economy was in a decline. There was much unemployment. The labor market was overcrowded. In the colonies, on the other hand, there was need for cheap labor. The British government decided to grant reprieves and stays of execution to convicted felons physically able to work so that they might be shipped abroad and impressed into service.

This system of deportation is part of the history of parole in that it involved mitigation of penal sentence and placement of the erstwhile prisoner in the free community. As in parole, the individual was not an altogether free person.

The first English transportation law was proclaimed in 1597, authorizing deportation of "rogues."

In 1619 one hundred "dissolute persons" were ordered to Virginia. The government paid a contractor, usually the shipmaster, about five pounds for each prisoner so shipped. In Virginia, the offenders were put up at auction, the highest bidder winning them as indentured servants. The British government thereafter exercised no further responsibility for the welfare or control of the former prisoners, so long as they did not return to England. If they returned without authorization, they were subject to death.

Boatloads of felons came over, but were not sufficient to meet the demand. Virginia thereupon began to import Negro slaves. The labor shortage eased, but the white exiles, despising their lot, fomented unrest among the blacks. This caused consternation among their masters, who could now get along without the transported convicts. Minus the white troublemakers, they could keep the slaves comfortably subjugated. Therefore, in 1670, the General Court at Jamestown announced that "because of the great number of felons and other desperate villains being sent over from the prisons of England, the horror yet remaining of the barbarous designs of those villains. . . . we do now prohibit the landing of any more jailbirds." [1]

It did Virginians little good to prohibit the practice. The British government was going to do as it pleased. Indeed, the deportation system was broadened. In 1717, under George I, an act read:

[1] Quoted in Margaret Wilson, *The Crime of Punishment* (New York: Harcourt, Brace & Co., 1931), p. 94.

Whereas in many of His Majesty's colonies. . . . in America, there
is great want of servants. . . . be it enacted that any person convicted of any offense for which he is liable to be whipt or burnt
on the hand, may be sent to some of his Majesty's Colonies in
America. Offenders returning before expiration of their term to be
liable to death.

Under this act, the contractor or shipmaster was given "property in the service" of a prisoner until the expiration of the
latter's term. When the felon's services were sold to a settler,
the "property in service" agreement was transferred. The trans-
portee, as in Virginia, became an indentured servant.

By 1775, the home country was transplanting some two thousand felons annually in the several colonies. The American
Revolution wrote finis to the practice.

But Australia was discovered, and in 1787 His Majesty announced he would send felons there as a means of exploiting
the land. A fantastic epoch in British history opened. Unlike
those sent to the American colonies, these deportees were not
to become indentured servants. The government would stand
the expense of shipping the prisoners and would continue
control over them in Australia, theoretically maintaining responsibility for their welfare and supervision over their conduct. Transported felons would remain prisoners. The governor of the penal settlement was to be given "property in
service." He could assign it to a free settler who would put
the prisoner to work. The settler gained the financial benefits
from such work, the prisoner obtaining from it only food and
shelter.

That prisoners did not want to go to Australia was of no
concern to His Majesty: Australia needed their labor. As the
Right Honorable William Eden pointed out in 1787, in his *In-
troductory Discourse on Banishment:*

Criminals have always been judged a fair subject of hazardous
experiments, to which it would be unjust to expose the more valua-

ble members of the state. If there be, therefore, any terrors in the prospect before the wretch who is banished to New South Wales, they are no more than he expects; if the dangers of a foreign climate be considered as nearly equivalent to death, the devoted convict naturally reflects that his crimes have drawn on this punishment, and that offended justice. . . . does not mean to seat him for life on a bed of roses.[2]

The first fleet of convicts set sail in May, 1787, under governor-designate Captain Arthur Phillip. In addition to the crew there were 552 males and 190 females aboard, a ratio productive of considerable disruption of discipline. En route, the seamen mutinied over living conditions. Prisoners rebelled because they did not want to be deported. They managed to manufacture spirituous liquor, and rocked the vessels with riotous, bawdy behavior.

The fleet reached Botany Bay on January 18, 1788. Phillip sent food ashore by his mariners; they devoured it and came back for more. He beached provisions by a contingent of convicts; they hid it for future use. The felons were ordered to land some cows. They left them on the beach and escaped into the jungle. Sheep were put ashore, only to be killed by lightning.

Phillip would have the sailors build a prison. They asserted they were not hired as builders. The convicts were mighty sure *they* were not going to erect their own jailhouse. Finally, a few huts were put up, pending erection of a prison enclosure.

Life on Botany Bay began. Famine succeeded famine in the next twenty years. The free settlers suffered as much as the convicts, and were the more frustrated when the latter refused to work. Phillip put some prisoners on Norfolk Island, since fishing was supposed to be plentiful there. The fish stopped biting. Seed brought by the contingent would not sprout.

All over the inhabited areas of Australia the convicts ca-

[2] *Ibid.*, pp. 102–3.

roused, fought among themselves, bore children, and obeyed
orders only when whipped or tortured. They did not want to
make a life for themselves in Australia. They wanted to go
home. Some tried to row boats to India, hoping to get to England from there. Others attempted to walk to China. Fifty of
their skeletons were found, years later.

These men and women, Phillip decided, did not even fear
death. The threat of invoking capital punishment for misbehavior was ineffectual. Phillip concluded that the greatest fear
in the mind of man was that he might be devoured. Therefore, he asked for authority, in cases of convicts guilty of murder or sodomy, to sell them to bush natives for meat. It is
doubtful that approval was received from the Home Office.

Phillip hoped he might gain some control over his charges
when, in 1790, he was empowered to remit sentences of prisoners whose work record and conduct warranted. They would
receive a grant of land and the equivalent of an absolute pardon. The prisoners laughed. The land they wanted was called
England.

Phillip gave up. In 1792 he asked to be relieved. A succes-
sion of governors followed, including the infamous Captain
Bligh, in 1806. The entire colony, free and criminal, rose
against him and held him prisoner until he could be shipped
home.

TICKET OF LEAVE

There followed a development directly related to parole as
we understand it today. Absolute pardons were abolished and
a conditional form substituted. It was called "ticket of leave,"
and was not the invention of Alexander Maconochie, as many
penologists have assumed. The ticket of leave antedated
Maconochie's arrival in Australia. It was a declaration, signed
by the colonial governor, excusing a convict from further government work and permitting him to live independently, but

within a circumscribed district. He was no longer a prisoner
in close confinement. He supported himself, the government
giving up that responsibility with the grant of ticket of leave.

Thus we had several of the elements of parole. In a vague,
rudimentary way, ticket of leave was envisaged as a treatment
program of sorts, the ticket specifying that the grant was for
the convict's "own advantage." It involved release from confinement after part of the sentence was served. Such release
was conditional, "during good behavior or until His Excel-
lency's further pleasure shall be made known." But there was
no government supervision of the ticket-of-leave recipient, and
nothing, of course, was done to counsel him or her, as would
be the policy in a modern parole program.

This system, inaugurated about 1800, solved few problems.
The prisoners still preferred England to Australia. In 1811 a
revised policy was instituted. Where, previously, ticket of leave
could be granted no matter how little of the sentence had been
served, now the regulation limited it to those who had worked
off a prescribed portion of their sentence. In 1821 the formula
for minima was more definitely delineated: prisoners serving
a seven-year term were eligible in four years; those with four-
teen-year sentences could earn ticket of leave in six years;
lifers might gain conditional liberty in eight years.

But the ticket-of-leave plan lay comparatively fallow until
Alexander Maconochie arrived in Australia. While he cannot
be credited with originating the ticket, he may be called the
"father" of parole more appropriately than any other person.

Alexander Maconochie, a captain in the Royal Navy, became
governor of Norfolk Island in 1840. He was convinced that
the depravity and demoralization he found were due as much
to administrators as to deportees. Living conditions were fright-
ful. Discipline was extremely severe. Maconochie determined
to help the convicts gain back their morale and self-respect.
He built schools and churches. He gave each prisoner a small

plot of ground for a garden. He encouraged reading by distributing books. He disagreed with his predecessors that the convicts were beyond redemption. He walked among them unaccompanied by the usual bodyguard, showing that he trusted them. They were impressed.

Maconochie's distinctive contribution to parole was the mark system, which he made an integral part of the ticket-of-leave program. Marks were the convicts' "wages." For good conduct and satisfactory work a prisoner earned a certain number of marks per week. With these "wages" he cut down his period of confinement and eventually was released on ticket of leave. If he misbehaved, he was not lashed, as previously was the rule. He forfeited marks instead, prolonging his imprisonment thereby.

Maconochie had struck on an idea that gave prisoners hope. They, and they alone, could reduce their sentences. They could hasten the day when they would be on ticket of leave. And when that time came, it was now understood, they might return to England. Declared Maconochie: "When a man keeps the key of his own prison, he is soon persuaded to fit it to the lock." [3] The prisoners responded.

An adjuvant of the mark system was Maconochie's gradations of servitude. He reasoned that prisoners were subjected to grave temptation if released from maximum custody immediately into the free community. Such sudden withdrawal of control often produced violent explosions as former inmates found themselves able to satisfy desires repressed for years. Maconochie introduced the men and women by degrees to responsibility for self in community life.

His gradations were: (1) strict custody; (2) labor in government gangs; (3) freedom within a prescribed area; (4) ticket of leave, which permitted the prisoner to live where he chose,

[3] Frederick H. Wines, *Punishment and Reformation* (New York: Thomas Y. Crowell & Co., 1895), p. 209.

but under prescribed conditions; (5) full restoration of liberty.

Here we have a treatment program in which an offender, after serving some time, was conditionally released. And there was now some conception of supervision of the holder of a ticket. There was, however, scarcely anything that could be dignified by the designation of "treatment" in the post-release period.

Maconochie returned to England after four years, and became governor of the Birmingham jail. His ideas came under closer observation in the home country. As for Australia, with the discovery of gold, free settlers arrived in hordes, and they resented the presence of convict-competitors. They demanded that the prisoners and ticket-of-leave holders be got out of the gold fields and off the continent. They threatened revolt if any more prisoners were sent to penal colonies in Australia. Transportation to Australia was suspended, then fully terminated in 1867. The program which began as an economic measure ended as such.

Ticket of leave now came into use in England as part of the penal system. Persons holding the ticket were free to move about as they pleased. They were supposed to comport themselves properly, but there was no supervisory force to see that they did. Former prisoners were under instructions to keep the police informed of their whereabouts, but if they failed to report, it was unlikely that punitive measures would follow, since there was no enforcement staff.

THE IRISH SYSTEM

Refinements were added to ticket of leave when Walter Crofton became head of the Irish prison system. As it happens, it was his ideas, partly borrowed from Maconochie, that most directly influenced penal thought in the United States. Walter Crofton, therefore, ranks as another pioneer of parole. He gave it what was known as the "Irish system."

Like Maconochie, Crofton viewed the prison sentence and ticket of leave as two facets of one program, designed to rehabilitate, not merely to punish. He more firmly established the stages of servitude. For about nine months a prisoner was in solitary confinement, on reduced diet and forced to do monotonous labor. Then he was assigned to public works, and began earning marks. His privileges increased. The third stage was served either in the institution at Lusk or at Smithfield and was centered on preparation for release. Here the prisoner worked without supervision. His privileges further increased. Finally, he was released when he had an approved job. He was then under somewhat more careful supervision than theretofore. In rural areas, releasees were supervised by police, but those residing in Dublin came under the jurisdiction of an Inspector of Released Prisoners, a civilian, who had a twofold function. He protected the community by checking as best he could on his charges and cooperating with police when suspicion developed. He also attempted to assist those whom he supervised. They reported to him. He helped them find jobs, visited their homes, checked employment. The first person to hold this post, the equivalent of today's parole officer, was James P. Organ. According to record, he was a tireless man indeed.

Now we had all the requisites of parole, including supervision, treatment, and a paid parole worker.

American Origins

The American colonies, it will be recalled, received felons via the British transportation system and made them indentured servants. Indenture, which goes back to sixteenth-century English law, is itself an antecedent of parole. Under this system, an individual was bound out to a master for a certain period, to be taught a trade while performing service for his sponsor. Originally, indenture was not planned as a program for the offender group. Rather, it was intended as a means of support and trade training for dependent persons. Benjamin Franklin was indentured to his brother at the age of twelve. The conditions of the agreement should interest us, since they resemble modern rules and regulations applied to probationers and parolees:

Taverns, inns or alehouses he shall not haunt. At cards or dice tables or any other unlawful game he shall not play. Matrimony he shall not contract nor from the services of his said master day or night absent himself.[4]

In time, indenture was adapted to penological needs. After juvenile offenders had served part of a term in correctional institutions they might be placed out. They were bound to masters, as was done with nonoffenders. The states at first assumed no responsibility for the supervision of such work-home arrangements. In the middle of the nineteenth century, however, New York set the beginning of a pattern by appointing a state agent to supervise the children and see to it they were not unduly exploited.

Reduction of sentence for "good time" was another step toward parole. We have seen how this was achieved under ticket of leave. In the United States, "good time" laws preceded parole. They are commonly referred to as "commutation" laws, for they commute the sentence, that is, lessen its severity, by legal formula.

Adults received definite, or determinate, sentences in the nineteenth century. A ten-year term meant ten years in jail. The prisoner served it all. Whether he behaved or not, worked or not, learned something or not, he could neither lengthen nor shorten his sentence. This created problems of prison discipline.

The New York legislature passed a commutation law in 1817, intended to alleviate the situation. It allowed time off the def-

---

[4] Carl Van Doren, *Benjamin Franklin* (New York: Macmillan, 1938), p. 13.

inite sentence for good conduct and work willingly performed. However, the law was not mandatory upon wardens, and was never actually employed in an institution of the state.

In 1821 Connecticut passed a commutation law applicable to workhouse inmates. This statute was used. Other states wrote similar laws.

But commutation was not parole. Those definite-sentence prisoners who profited from it were released earlier, but unconditionally as a rule, and without supervision.

Parole works most effectively when the sentence is an indeterminate one. A truly indeterminate term would specify neither minimum nor maximum limits, leaving these to the discretion of a stated authority. We have no such sentence in the United States. We do have what is called an "indeterminate" term, but it always specifies a maximum and almost always a minimum. However, a prisoner is able to shorten his period of incarceration under the indeterminate sentence. If released ahead of his maximum, he still "owes" part of the sentence and can be placed under parole supervision. The flexibility of the indeterminate sentence is a strong psychological factor in parole.

The principle of the indeterminate sentence was first employed in a New York State enactment of 1824, applying exclusively to juveniles. But not until the same state erected the reformatory at Elmira was this country to have an indeterminate sentence for adults. And with the creation of the New York State Reformatory at Elmira we were to build into its program the first parole system in the United States.

Elmira Reformatory was a product of the times, an outcropping of the reformatory movement. Penologists had fretted for years over the failure of the prison system. What was needed, progressives insisted, was an institution based upon a new premise. It would deemphasize punishment for the sake of punishment and substitute reeducation of the offender. Reformatories would reform, meaning reshape, human beings.

The reformatory movement first took root in the Eastern United States. Franklin Benjamin Sanborn, secretary of the Board of State Charities of Massachusetts, issued a report in 1865 describing the Maconochie and Crofton ticket-of-leave systems. It played a part in the decision to erect the Elmira Reformatory.

It was proposed to build an institution for young adults with reformation as the goal and with some provision for aftercare upon their release. Elmira opened its doors in July, 1876. It was not envisaged as a maximum security prison, but retained some of the physical features of such edifices nevertheless. There were barred cells, locked corridors, the standard safe custody provisions. The great departure was in program. The first superintendent was Zebulon R. Brockway. An experienced and progressive penologist, he set the tone of Elmira Reformatory.

The age range for commitment was sixteen to thirty. Only defendants never before convicted of felony were eligible for reception at Elmira. The principles behind the institution are worth study. Enunciated by the founders, they contributed to parole philosophy in the United States:

1. Offenders are reformable. This simple assertion is the core of parole philosophy. If people cannot be helped to change for the better, why spend money on parole?

2. Reformation is the right of every convict and the duty of the state. Revolutionary doctrine! Most people felt that criminals had no rights and the one duty of the state was to punish them.

3. Every prisoner must be individualized. The emphasis would be upon the offender, not the offense.

4. Time must be given the reformatory process to take effect. If faith in Elmira was justified, if it had something to offer, then the emphasis should not be upon rushing a man out, but

on helping him get the maximum benefits while he is inside. Teaching a trade, schooling, treating attitudes—these would take time.

5. The prisoner's cure is always facilitated by his cooperation and often impossible without it. Today, we are chary of the word "cure" in this context, for we are not sure whether or when it has been effected. Nevertheless, contemporary penologists approve the general principle.

6. No other form of reward and punishment is so effective as transfer from one custodial class to another, with different privileges in each, but the most important agency for gaining a prisoner's cooperation is the power possessed by the administrators to lengthen or shorten the term of incarceration. That called for a program of parole. At Elmira, it was patterned on the Irish system.

7. Finally, the reformatory process is educational. That means more than instructional. It includes the concept of re-education of attitudes, motivation, behavior.

Elmira made use of the mark system, grades of incarceration, the indeterminate sentence, and conditional release— called parole. While the parole system was fashioned on Crofton's, it underscored more than he did the necessity for adequate supervision of parolees by competent personnel.

Parole and the indeterminate sentence spread from Elmira to other institutions in the state, and from New York into other parts of the country. By 1891, eight states had authorized the indeterminate sentence, but only for first offenders (except in New York State).[5] Today it is much more widespread and inclusive. Every state except Vermont now has statutory provision for both juvenile and adult parole. The Federal courts use a definite sentence in adult cases, but by operation of "good time" laws, prisoners may be released and placed under supervision before the full term is served.

[5] And in New York, women were excluded from its benefits!

Variations in Pattern

In 1941 the American Law Institute issued a Model Youth Correction Act, which proposed the creation of a Youth Authority in each state to integrate all work with young offenders from time of adjudication to final discharge. The court would commit to the Authority rather than to a specific institution. The Authority would examine and test the committed youth, assign him to an appropriate institution, supervise the program there, sit as a parole board to select inmates for release, and direct the parole function and field workers supervising parolees. From beginning to end, one Authority would follow the case.

In 1941 California led the way by setting up its Youth Correction Authority, later named the Youth Authority. Minnesota followed, then Wisconsin, Massachusetts, Texas, Kentucky, Illinois, Washington, and the Federal Government.

In California the administrative functions of the Youth Authority are vested in the Director of the Department of the Youth Authority. He is also chairman of the Youth Authority Board. The Board, as such, has no administrative powers over management of the institutions, nor does it direct the parole service. It is a term-fixing and paroling agency, but firm liaison with other functions exists because the administrator, that is, the Director of the department, is a member of the Board and its chairman.

This separation of policy determination and administration is viewed by many as an improvement over the provisions of the original Model Act, which vested both functions in one board. It is generally held that broad policy-making and quasi-judicial functions are proper spheres for boards, but that day-to-day administration and management are best handled by a single administrator, properly controlled in law and supported by competent staff.

This separation of administration and policy formulation was not provided for when, in 1944, California went a step further and established its Adult Authority on much the same basis as its Youth Authority, with jurisdiction over adult males. The law setting up the Adult Authority also revamped the state-level correctional system generally. It provided for a Department of Corrections, of which the Adult Authority was nominally a part. There was to be a Director of Corrections, responsible to the governor. In him was vested most of the administrative responsibilities for operating the department, with the exception of transfers between institutions and supervision of the field parole agents of the Division of Adult Paroles. The Adult Authority was assigned certain "functional" supervisory powers over some of the activities which were the administrative responsibilities of the Director. These included the classification of inmates in the institutions, reception and diagnostic clinic activities, and prison discipline. It will be apparent to the reader that the distinction between administration (the Director's job) and policy-making plus quasi-judicial functions of the Adult Authority was somewhat clouded. The Adult Authority Board was itself charged with "functional" supervisory powers which were administrative in nature.

From the beginning, therefore, it was necessary to enter into an extralegal agreement between the Adult Authority and the Director with respect to classification, discipline, and reception procedures. The management of these activities became the full responsibility of the Director, along with other administrative duties. The Adult Authority entered into certain matters in an advisory capacity.

In 1953 there came an attempt at legal clarification. The law was amended to remove from the province of the Adult Authority all those activities carried on within the institutions. They were transferred completely to the jurisdiction of the Director. Left in the law was reference to the concept that the

Director should consult with the Adult Authority in matters of policy with respect to these functions. He was not, however, finally bound by their advice.

In 1957 the statute was further amended, transferring the management of the Division of Adult Paroles from the Board of the Adult Authority to the Director of Corrections. Now the Division of Adult Paroles has the same relationship to the Director as has each of the institutions. Its head is appointed by him and responsible to him.

California's state-level correctional program for adults now operates much the same as does the Youth Authority, except that the Director of Corrections is not a member of the Adult Authority. The latter has the same powers, generally, as the Youth Authority. It fixes the minimum time to be served and decides who shall be granted parole. The law provides, however, that the Director of Corrections shall meet with the Adult Authority six times a year while they are fixing terms and granting paroles. This has the effect of requiring that the Director and the Adult Authority work closely in matters in which they have a mutual interest.

The Adult Authority emerges, with these statutory amendments, as the term-fixing body (within statutory limits). It also grants and revokes parole.

Rationale of Parole

Why parole prisoners at all? Many ask this, and some are convinced the answer should be, "Why, indeed?"

The use of parole is sound social economy. It benefits the public as well as the parolee. In fact, the alternative—no parole —would subject us to danger.

Consider this: Ninety-five percent of adult prisoners must someday come out of jail. Probably 99 percent of juvenile delinquents leave correctional institutions after a comparatively short stay. The few prisoners who do not come out are executed or die of natural causes. All the others must sometime finish their sentences. Is it not to our interest to see to it that those released come under supervision for some time, as they reaccustom themselves to life outside?

If we accept this premise, that it is better for all released prisoners to be under supervision for a period, we can go a step further in our rationale. We must assume, as we do with probationers, that a great many prisoners are susceptible to change. Assuming (for the sake of discussion) that the institution does something to help bring this about, there comes a time when an inmate has profited as much as he ever will from incarceration. At that psychological moment, if we can capture it, we should parole him. To retain him further would be to countervail both the community's and the individual's welfare.

This was well stated by Convict 1776 in his autobiography:

Life in prison is absolutely artificial. A very short time in isolated confinement is ample for all needed introspection and retrospection. Then such confinement begins insidiously to attack the prisoner; it affects his body, his mind, his very soul, until he is unfit for freedom. Consequently it should never be continued longer than is necessary for the prisoner to gain a sane conception of his duties to you and a desire to perform them.[6]

Purposeless confinement, Convict 1776 is saying, causes inmates to lose the gains they may have made. It hardens and embitters them, leaves them the more inaccessible to those who would help them become law-abiding.

Prisoners should not be merely released. They should be paroled, under the care and supervision society wants them to have in its own interest.

Aims of Parole

The aims of parole are implicit in what we have said. They are exactly the same as those of probation. We want to help

[6] Anonymous, *An Open Letter to Society from Convict 1776* (New York: Fleming H. Revell Co., 1911), p. 159.

erstwhile offenders find their way back into society, where they may live more comfortably with themselves and others than they did before they were convicted. We want to furnish society, at the same time, protection against the potential recidivist.

5

PAROLE TODAY

There are state parole systems, with jurisdiction over persons in state correctional institutions eligible for parole. This is the predominant form of organization. Additionally, there are county and municipal units, with jurisdiction in their respective levels of institutions. There is a Federal parole system for individuals released from penitentiaries and reformatories under the control of the National Government.

As has been stated, there is a trend toward a combined, statewide probation and parole service for all but Federal cases. Florida, Mississippi, Maine, Missouri, and Kansas are among those with such plan of administration.

Eligibility for Parole

When does an inmate become eligible for parole? There is great diversity of pattern. Juveniles may usually be released at the discretion of the paroling authority. Sentences to reformatories for young adults are also likely to be flexible. Prison sentences are subject to more restrictive statutes.

Some prisoners—the relatively few who are serving straight life terms—will never be eligible for parole. Some states additionally rule out persons convicted of certain offenses, such as murder, rape, incest, and kidnaping. These inmates will not be eligible for parole, although they may come out of prison eventually, by action of a governor or by service of the maximum sentence. Another basis of exclusion from parole is prior conviction of felony. While the majority of states make it possible for an inmate with a prior felony record to gain parole, a few make him ineligible.

Blanket restrictions on eligibility, as we have noted, contradict the principle of individualization. Even where murder is concerned, there is a difference between the hired killer and the man or woman who commits a crime of passion. The latter makes the best possible parole risk, research indicates. Yet the law may proscribe release for such an inmate.

In addition to denying parole to certain categories of offenders altogether, most states specify the minimum time to be served before eligibility occurs for those who may be considered.

1. It might be the minimum of the sentence less good time allowance. For example, if the sentence is five to ten years, the prisoner is eligible in five years less the time he earns for good behavior and work willingly performed.

2. It might be a specified part of the maximum. Some laws require service of half the maximum; others, one third; and so on.

3. There are many other formulas. There may be, for instance, a one year minimum, regardless of the maximum; or one third of the term or ten years, whichever is less. A Federal prisoner (other than a juvenile delinquent or youthful offender), if serving more than 180 days, is eligible for parole after completing one third of the sentence. When a life sentence is imposed by a Federal court, the earliest possible release is in fifteen years.

If we rule out of consideration the states setting no eligibility limitations, we have a refutation for critics who cry that "the judges send them away for long terms and the parole boards turn them loose before the sentence is legally served." The plain fact is that a board can never release a prisoner before he has served the minimum sentence specified in law. He must complete that. Moreover, very often the board does not parole at minimum eligibility. In other words, a board can cause an inmate to serve more than the minimum, but it cannot release him earlier than the law provides.

Parole-granting Agency

Who grants parole?

There are three types of parole-granting agencies: the institutional board; the central parole board; and a body of public officials whose principal functions are other than parole granting.[1]

An institutional board is composed mainly, sometimes exclusively, of personnel from the specific prison or reformatory. The warden or superintendent will almost certainly sit on it and be like Milton's ladies, "whose bright eyes/Rain influence." Other members may include a chaplain, disciplinarian, educational director, or psychiatrist.

Proponents of such boards hold they have an advantage over the central authority. Institutional people, they assert, understand inmates. Prisoner Jones may "con" an outsider, but not the "screw," the "bug doctor," or the warden. Personnel can assess an inmate's dossier more realistically than would someone unfamiliar with intramural life.

Opponents of the institutional plan aver that prison and reformatory staffs do, indeed, know inmates, since they mingle with them constantly. That very fact, they claim, may produce bias. And while institutional dossiers are valuable, they could be made available to an outside parole board, along with interpretation.

The institutional plan seems unsound administratively where there is more than one correctional establishment in the state. Suppose we have ten prisons. That means ten boards, ten standards of operation. It means, as a rule, that parole officers

[1] In a few instances, paroles from city and county institutions are granted by the court of conviction.

from ten prisons cover the same territory. A central plan of administration would save a great amount of money.

An institutional board is likely to bow to the warden or superintendent. And he would be less than human if he did not consider certain institutional problems in their relation to parole. When the inmate population rises, he may urge, "Get them out! We're sleeping them in the corridors!" Parole should be based upon no such extraneous consideration.

The central parole board consists of one body which meets in all the institutions of the given jurisdiction to pass on paroles. This form of organization received the nod from the 1956 National Conference on Parole, when Workshop II, on sentencing and parole laws, declared that an effective parole law should, among other specifications, provide for a central paroling agency.

The third type of parole authority, composed of part-time public officials, is a haphazard, catch-as-catch-can body— fortunately in a distinct minority. A governor, his attorney general, and/or other officials pass on releases. Obviously, each is too preoccupied with other duties to give to selection for parole the painstaking study it requires.

In the majority of state jurisdictions, parole board members are appointed by the governor, with the consent of one or both houses of legislature. In Florida, Michigan, and Wisconsin they are selected by merit system examination. In several jurisdictions a director of public welfare, a board of correction, or the state supreme court makes the selection. Occasionally, a governor empowered to appoint asks appropriate public and private organizations to present him with a panel of acceptable candidates, from which he will make his selection.

Should parole board members be appointees or career officials?

There are arguments on both sides of the question. A governor, say some, should have the right to select his top policymakers, relying on their performance record or discharging them if he cannot sustain their decisions. If he is held responsible by the public for the acts of his top department heads, as is usual, this may stimulate him to appoint the most capable persons possible.

Those defending the negative in this debate assert that too often a chief executive makes appointments with one eye cocked at the political horizon, the other at his relatives. A merit system discourages the chief executive who would play politics with parole. It brings in careerists with no political obligations, no fences to build or repair, no logs to roll. It creates tenure, continuity of service, and consistency of operation.

However selected, membership on boards runs from one to ten. The qualifications desired are set forth in law only vaguely. Members might be expected to be "persons of good moral character," a semantic teaser challenging any appointing body. In California, the law is more specific. Members of the Adult Authority shall have "a broad background in and ability for appraisal of law offenders and the circumstances of the offense for which convicted." While that specification presents its difficulties in interpretation, the law goes on to say that in so far as practicable, members "shall be selected who have a varied and sympathetic interest in corrections work including persons widely experienced in the fields of corrections, sociology, law, law enforcement, and education." [2]

Some statutes stipulate that the board member, after appointment, shall not engage in political activity or hold public office. Some provide that he or she must hold no other employment, engage in no business, and devote full time to official parole duties.

Tenure of board members runs from "pleasure of the governor" to a maximum of ten years. Members may usually be

[2] Sec. 5075, *California Penal Code.*

reappointed. Four- and six-year terms seem to be the most common.

There is great diversification in salary, running from as low as $10 per diem to a high in the neighborhood of $17,000 annually.

Parole Supervision

Who supervises parole?

Under the institutional parole board plan, field agents from the given prison or reformatory usually supervise those released therefrom. The central board has its own field staff, serving all the institutions and releasees.

Revocation

The paroling body has the final authority to revoke parole.[3] It has been consistently held that such determinations are not reviewable by the courts.

Discharge

Eligibility for discharge follows two patterns with adults. In some jurisdictions parolees are required to serve the difference between time served in the institution and the maximum of the sentence. For example, Tom is sentenced to a seven-and-a-half to fifteen-year term. He serves eight years, is paroled. He has seven more years to do on parole.

In other systems, the parole-granting agency may, at its discretion, fix a term less than the maximum sentence. Tom might then be told that if his behavior is satisfactory he will be discharged from parole in, say, three years.

No statute permits extension of the parole period beyond the maximum sentence.

For juvenile offenders, the law permits the utmost flexibility.

[3] Except in Texas, where such authority rests with the governor by constitutional provision.

Discharge may come soon after release or it may not be granted until majority has been attained, practice in individual cases, even within the same parole unit, running the gamut. In rare instances, it is legally possible to retain juveniles on parole past their majority.

Status of Parole

Parole, like probation, has made progress. It has not achieved all its goals. As the Superintendent of Parole Supervision of the Pennsylvania Board of Parole put it, "A broad view of parole today, compared with the view fifty years ago, should give us a feeling of satisfaction, but scarcely justifies complacency." [4]

The Parole Process

Now, as we did with probation, let us follow the parole process from beginning to end.

James Carter was sentenced to state prison for a term of five to ten years for armed robbery. He is a first felony offender. In his state he is required to serve "minimum less compensation" ("good time") before becoming eligible for parole. Let us say he will be eligible in three and a half years.

We will also assume a situation in which parole staff is stationed in the prison. The parole officer will give Carter certain information about his possible future release. He will do this shortly after the prisoner's admission. Carter will learn what parole is, what it expects, and what it offers. Later on, Carter will receive more detailed instruction on preparation to meet the parole board, how to locate a job offer, what the rules will be if he is released, and other matters.

Now Carter is three months short of minimum eligibility. Again we hypothecate a reasonably effective level of operation. A parole officer goes into the field and prepares a preparole

[4] G. I. Giardini, "Adult Parole," *National Probation and Parole Journal.* III (1957), 381.

investigation report, consisting of a rounded social history of the inmate and including a home and employment program.

The parole board meets in the prison, reads the report, and interviews Carter. It denies him parole, specifying it will see him again in six months. If he comes out at that time, he will have served four full years.

At the stipulated time, a rehearing is held. This time Carter "makes" parole. He comes out owing six years. We will postulate he is in a state which automatically requires he serve the full balance on parole.

Carter makes his arrival report within twenty-four hours after leaving prison, meets his parole officer, is instructed in the rules and regulations, and given to understand what he may and may not expect of the agency. Chances are he is at least as distrustful of the officer as a probationer would be.

He reports regularly; the officer visits home, employment, wherever else is indicated. Carter gradually lets down his guard, learns to respect his parole officer, perhaps even to like him. (Another parolee might never develop this far, continuing to distrust and be evasive with the officer.)

Carter spends six uneventful years on parole, is discharged from supervision. Should he commit a felony an hour after his parole period expired, he cannot be held to account for the earlier term.

Let us say Carter is paroled after serving four years. He remains in good standing for a year, then absconds. The officer prepares a violation of parole report; the absconder is declared delinquent. His time stops running. He owes five years and will continue to owe it no matter when apprehended.

He is picked up six years after declaration of delinquency and returned to prison owing five years. (The delinquency could, of course, have been canceled, in which case he would be restored to parole standing. This would automatically discharge Carter from parole, for he would have restored to him, as if served in good standing, the time between date of declaration of delinquency and date of cancellation.)

Back in prison, Carter is assessed two years of penalty time by the parole board. That means he may be reparoled.

But he misbehaves, and when he appears before the board once more, is held one more year. He serves the additional year and is accorded another hearing. He owed five years upon return as a violator. He has served three of the five. When the parole board reparoles him, he owes another two years.

He concludes his parole period satisfactorily this time and is discharged.

Carter came out in four years originally, served a year under supervision, then behaved in a manner to warrant the suspicion he was on the way to becoming a violator.

An investigation is conducted. The suspicion is borne out. The officer prepares a violation report. The board decides to give Carter another chance. It continues him under supervision. He has lost no credit for time served to now.

But suppose the board did declare Carter delinquent and ordered him back to prison. Then he comes in owing five years. The board may give him any or all of that time.

Say Carter, on parole, is convicted of another felony. He might be in a state where the parole authority must cause him to serve all his unexpired time before beginning service of the second sentence. Having come out originally owing six years, no matter how long he remained in good standing, he now must serve six years in prison (less "good time") before beginning service of the second term. But if the board has discretion in the matter, it might assess him only a portion of the first sentence, then parole him to start serving the second.

We will now consider the case of Mary, a juvenile, adjudged a delinquent when she ran away from home and was found to be sexually promiscuous. She is sent to a correctional school. We will act on the assumption that in her state she may be retained until she is twenty-one. She is sixteen upon admission.

Procedures are informal here. The parole authority may consider Mary's release at any time. A year after her reception, she has changed so much and so favorably that the board, after a field investigation, paroles her. She is to live with her parents. She is told she will be on parole for two years, although the board could keep her under supervision for four years if it chose.

Mary meets her parole officer, almost certainly a woman. The girl is likely to become quite attached to the officer. Girls seem to relate to their parole officers more readily than boys at this age.

On the other hand, if the officer lacks tact, warmth, or skill, Mary may develop strong dislike for her supervisor and, unlike an adult with more self-control, erupt angrily, abscond, or withhold important information.

But if the officer is reasonably perceptive she can gain Mary's confidence. She will also understand that at that age, the girl is subject to certain hazards. It might be a sudden crush on a boy who can do her no good, a temper tantrum at home or in the office. The parole officer, without condoning foolish behavior, will make clear by her attitude that she will tolerate a certain amount of misconduct, if not too serious. She wants Mary to feel free to discuss her feelings and problems. Were the officer a martinet, forgiving no minor slip, the parolee would retreat into herself.

Suppose Mary, with two years to do on parole, conducts herself only halfway satisfactorily. The parole authority has the power to return her to the institution or to extend her parole period, up to her majority.

Should Mary do exceptionally well, the supervision period may be shortened.

Let us assume that after a year on parole, Mary is found to be cohabiting with a man, and withholding this information from the parole officer. The board may return her to the correctional school and keep her there as long as it deems necessary, up to but not exceeding her majority.

Mary, on parole, is adjudged a delinquent again. After the juvenile court has acted on the new offense, the parole body may affix penalty time on the old adjudication. Or it may decline to do so, having discretion in the matter.

Whatever happens, however many times Mary is adjudicated a delinquent, no matter how many parole periods she has served, when she reaches the age of twenty-one, she will, by the laws of her state, be discharged finally from parole obligations.

The Question of Civil Rights

A word about the complicated matter of civil rights as they are affected by criminal offense. This is a subject of vital importance to the parolee. Under our theory of the State, a person's rights are supreme. He may not be deprived of them except by due process of law.

An individual is deprived of his freedom when he is sentenced to a penal institution, but this is by due process. He has had a trial, under prescribed legal procedures.

A defendant in a criminal action may be deprived of life, this, too, by due process of law.

Such adjudications are individually imposed, on the basis of facts disclosed in court proceedings. There are other, general, rights lost by all individuals upon conviction, under our con-stitutions and penal codes. These losses, too, occur only after due process, that is, legal conviction and subsequent sentence. They apply to the entire aggregation of convicted persons. The judge has no discretion in the matter. The fact of conviction and imprisonment under certain circumstances in itself makes mandatory the revocation of certain rights. Those certain circumstances, for the most part, have to do with the length of period of incarceration and place where the time is served. For instance, the law usually invokes the disprivilege only upon conviction of a felony in which the defendant serves more than one year in a state prison.

The disprivileged offender is not deprived of citizenship.[5] His property rights are in general secure, except as statutes may limit them. That is, in the absence of contravening law, the convict may take, hold, and dispose of his property by will, deed, or other method. In almost every state a convicted felon may testify in a court proceeding, although, of course, his credibility as a witness may be challenged.

What rights *are* lost?

In all but five states—Arizona, Michigan, New Hampshire, Pennsylvania, and Vermont—the convict loses the franchise.

In Illinois, Missouri, Montana, Nebraska, Ohio, and Wyoming he is disqualified for jury duty. In most states he is denied the right to hold public office. In some jurisdictions he loses the right to take civil service examinations.

Conviction of a felony with sentence to imprisonment is a ground for divorce in thirty-five states.

A person who has lost his civil rights may not bring a lawsuit, although he may be sued, in which case he has a right to defend himself.

[5] But the United States Code, Title 8, section 801, provides that upon conviction for treason, attempting to overthrow or bear arms against the United States, or conviction by a court martial on a charge of desertion in time of war from the military or naval service of the United States, citizenship is forfeited.

There is a difference of legal interpretation as to whether an insurance policy on the life of an executed offender needs to be paid.

In New York State, the convict who has suffered forfeiture of civil rights loses some of his natural rights as a parent. For instance, his children may be offered for adoption and adopted without his consent.

Seventeen states provide that a defendant sentenced to a life term shall be deemed civilly dead. In seven states, the statutes permit distribution of the civilly dead convict's property as though he were naturally dead. Civil death dissolves the convict's marriage although that same "dead" person is still obligated to support his dependants!

In general, such rights as are not specifically revoked by law are deemed to be retained by the offender.[6]

Are civil rights forfeited where a defendant, although convicted, has been given a suspended sentence? In many such cases, courts have ruled they are not.

A juvenile adjudged a delinquent never loses his civil rights, whatever the disposition of his case.

Misdemeanants usually retain their rights upon conviction.

The statutes are strictly construed. Where the law speaks of prisons or penitentiaries, a commitment to a reformatory does not entail loss of rights.

Despite rigid interpretation, however, there is still some confusion and difference of interpretation as to particular rights lost in given states, the point at which they are forfeited, and whether and how they may be restored. It will be appreciated that these disprivileges can so handicap an individual as to make it difficult for him to live honestly after release. Therefore, either the law must find a remedy or law enforcement must wink at violators. We choose, of course, to offer remedies.

[6] For most of the material given here on loss of civil rights I am deeply indebted to Sol Rubin, counsel to the National Probation and Parole Association.

6

PROBATION AND PAROLE:
COMPANION SERVICES

Having examined the historical and philosophical backgrounds of probation and parole, we may now inquire more closely into the nature of these services. What *are* probation and parole?

Let us approach an answer by first making clear what they are *not*, for there is much confusion in the matter. Public and press are prone to think that anyone with a criminal record must *ipso facto* be a probationer or parolee.

An individual may be fined for his offense and set at liberty. He is not a probationer. Neither is the person who receives a suspended sentence with no stipulation for supervision. Sentences may be suspended without the imposition of a probation term.

The prisoner pardoned by a governor is the beneficiary of executive clemency, not parole. Another inmate may be serving a definite sentence. He will do it all, minus such "good time" as the statute provides. He comes out, not by action of a parole board, but by mandatory features of law.

A man or woman serving an indeterminate sentence may be denied parole when eligible and required to serve the full maximum of his or her term. That person would leave the institution, not as a parolee, but as a free person, released by law and not by action of a parole authority.

And, of course, many people who come to public attention

One remedy is executive clemency in the form of a pardon to remove disability and restore all or certain civil rights. A more recent development has been the certificate of rehabilitation, also given other titles. The certificate is commonly issued by a parole authority or judge, as the law may direct. The governor usually must approve before the certificate may be issued.

because they commit crimes were once on probation or parole, but finished their terms and were discharged. They were not under supervision when they got into further difficulties and they cannot properly be classed as probationers or parolees.

Obviously, a probationer is an offender placed in his status by a court. A parolee is one who left a correctional institution by action of a parole board. Both court and parole agency had other legal alternatives available.

Each individual concerned is a probationer or parolee so long as his supervision period has not expired or been terminated by revocation.

Differences and Similarities

The essential difference between the two programs is that the parolee has served part of his term in a correctional establishment and will do the balance or some part of it outside, while the probationer does all his time in the community, with no prior incarceration for the offense.

Some persons in the field believe there is another difference. The parolee, they assert, is likely to be more hardened and embittered than the probationer, hence less responsive to treatment. He has, after all, served in an institution.

The present writer feels there is so little contrast between a probationer and a parolee that practically anything said about one supervisory service may with equal validity be asserted about the other. Case records reveal that a great many juvenile and adult probationers *have* had a prior institutional experience. Moreover, we cannot hold that all correctional institutions invariably have a destructive effect upon every inmate. Further, it is conceivable that a probationer who was never in an institution may yet be as resistant to the authority of society as a parolee who has served a long term.

For example, here is an excerpt from a tape recording of an interview by the author with a young man, then seventeen, a

juvenile by the laws of his state. Member of a street gang, Roy
was in constant trouble with the law. However, he never served
a reformatory term. He did have a brief probation period, for
drunken driving, without a license, in a stolen car, in the course
of which he ran into a dwelling, seriously injuring the occupant.

Q: You've been to Juvenile Court, haven't you?
A: Oh, yeah! A few times. The only thing I don't go for is Juvenile
Court. I don't like that for the birds. You can't say anything to
defend yourself. All they say is, this petition filed against you on
such and such a day, it says you done such and such a thing. Well,
we're gonna hold you for so long. Or, I'm gonna send you to the
ref, or something. There's nobody to defend you, nothing like that.
It just says you did it, you're gonna go away. For Chrissake! Them
Juvenile Court judges, they don't know a goddamn thing, just want
to get it over with. Bang! Just shove them poor kids in the can!
Q: How about cops?
A: Aw! They start giving you a bad time the minute they get that
badge. Rookie cops, they just get on the force and they want to
be sergeant right away. Yeah. There's a lot of cops that give you
a rough time. They would haul you in for everything. Like if they
see you with a can of beer, they don't say, "Well, as long as
you're only drinking beer, well, go ahead." If I was a cop I'd rather
see a kid sitting around with a can of beer than I would with a
marijuana cigarette, something like that. Cops!
Q: Your friend Carl, his father is worth millions. How come he
pals around with you guys?
A: Because he's regular, he ain't chicken, he wants to be around
decent guys, not some jerk that's gonna stay home and toast marsh-
mallows. He knows we take to him.
Q: Why do you take to him?
A: What I mean, this Carl, where his father could buy him a
whole new car if he wanted one, when he wants hub caps, he don't
go out and buy them. He goes out and steals them, off some car
parked at night.
Q: The rest of you expect that of him? Is that what you mean?
A: No. He expects it of himself. Because he wants to be like other
fellows. It would be like Bing Crosby. He's got a name for being
rich. He surely wouldn't run around in ragged dungarees, in a
Model A. He'd live up to the name that he's got money.

Q: Carl has money. Why doesn't he live up to his name by buying his hub caps instead of stealing them?

A: Because he wants to live up to the gang, like you or me would.

Q: Has everybody got a right to hold on to his own property?

A: Sure. I think so.

Q: Then why do some people steal that property?

A: I don't know. I don't know what the hell they want to do that for.

Q: But you've done it.

A: Yeah.

Q: Well? You know it's wrong but you do it. Why?

A: Everybody else is gonna do it, you might as well do it, too.

[Roy and his gang stood by as some teen-agers cut and stabbed a boy with razors and knives, tied him to a car bumper and rammed him into a stone fence, bashing in his skull and killing him.]

Q: Do you think a gang is ever justified in killing a fellow?

A: Oh, yeah! I do.

Q: Under what circumstances?

A: When a guy can't keep his mouth shut about something that's really dangerous.

Q: I see. Any other time when it's O.K. to kill a guy?

A: Yeah. I'd justify myself in killing a cop that got smart. Well, yeah! I might not get away with it, but I'd sure try like hell if he got smart.

Q: Roy, you've been given advice by your folks on staying out of trouble. Mr. ——, down in the Juvenile Detail, has tried to help you. You don't have anything nice to say about him, and mighty little, for that matter, about your folks, except maybe your father. You don't like cops, you don't like judges. You didn't like your probation officer. Now, all these people wanted to see you stay out of trouble. You've got no use for them?

A: It ain't that. All I want is they should keep their nose out. There ain't a one of them that knows what I want. Nobody can tell you what you want to do except yourself. I level with my Dad most of the time, because he don't tell me what to do. These cops and things, they been reading books about crime that was written by college professors. What the hell do them college professors know about us kids?

This young man has demonstrated that he means what he says. He has committed rape, robbery, burglary, assault, and other offenses. Police believe he probably is guilty of at least one murder. He is inured to antisocial acts. He fulminates against law enforcement officers. Yet he has never been in a correctional institution.

The point is that many probationers, although of course not all, are tough, antisocial in their attitudes. So are some, but not all, parolees. Some probationers are tougher than parolees and vice versa. The differential may or may not be a prison or reformatory experience. "Parolees and probationers are people. Each one is conditioned by his particular make-up, experiences, and response to environment." [1]

A probation caseload is not likely to be of markedly different character from a parole load. The service needs will be very much the same, as will the techniques for meeting those needs.

Casework? Law Enforcement?

All right. Probation and parole are basically alike. What are they? Casework? Law enforcement? Both? Neither? You can start a heated argument on this wherever correctional workers gather.

Some say probation and parole are casework services, one kind of social work practice and altogether divorced from law enforcement.[2] Others would as vehemently vouchsafe that these are law enforcement functions exclusively and caseworkers should be kept away with an eleven-foot pole. Another segment of opinion maintains that probation and parole are casework *and* law enforcement, one coming into play when the other is no longer effective. And still another group would declare: "A plague o' all your houses! We're not social workers

---

[1] Dressler, *Probation and Parole*, pp. 14–15.

[2] We shall be discussing social casework later on, but so we may have the same point of reference, let us for the present use this definition, to be found in Helen Harris Perlman, *Social Casework, a Problem-solving Process* (Chicago: University of Chicago Press, 1957), p. 4: "Social casework is a process used by certain human welfare agencies to help individuals to cope more effectively with their problems in social functioning."

and we aren't policemen. We are a highly specialized and unique practice, different from any other concerned with human relations."

Then, too, there are those who insist this is a service calling for no specialization whatever. Probation and parole are unrelated to any discipline or practice that relies upon the scientific approach, according to proponents of this viewpoint. They are just plain common sense with no frills attached. The less science and "red tape," the better. Anyone with a good heart, or a big stick, depending upon the speaker, can do probation and parole work.

Where lies reality?

In terms of actual practice, everywhere. Somewhere, in some jurisdiction, we find each point of view translated into practice.

But what can we reasonably assert probation and parole ought to be? The author expresses his personal opinion here, reminding the reader that many responsible correctional workers would not share his views.

Probation and parole are social work. *Social work*, not exclusively *casework*. Social work encompasses the several fields of group work, casework, and community organization. Casework plays the greatest part in treatment in correctional settings, but group work and community welfare organization have their role too.

Like all of social work, probation and parole adapt generic principles to their specific objectives and functions. A public assistance agency is a casework organization, but some of its approaches and emphases differ from those in a private family service agency, which also practices casework. A community center is a group work agency, but some of its operations are unlike those found in a settlement house, another group work undertaking. Probation and parole make their adaptations, utilizing whatever is of value anywhere in all the fields of social work.

With regard to the law enforcement *vs.* social work argument, it seems to this writer we need make no choice, in correctional work. We require both. We cannot divorce ourselves from the enforcement function, and it ill behooves us to derogate it. Courts and parole boards are charged with selecting for treatment only those calculated to be reasonably safe risks. Probation and parole officers take an oath of office as peace officers. The legislative intent is obvious here. Officers are enjoined to protect the community.

The writer disagrees with those who asseverate that probation and parole are neither law enforcement nor social work, but something uniquely special.[3] He rejects the proposition that probation and parole require no more than common sense, while cheerfully agreeing that common sense is one ingredient essential to practically any undertaking. It tells me my plumbing leaks. But it takes a plumber's skill *and* common sense to fix it. The human being is infinitely more complex than a water faucet. He requires a highly specialized and expertly trained practitioner to help him with his multifarious personal problems. That person must have common sense. But common sense without professional skill can work to the detriment of the individual seeking help.

This, then, is the bias of the author, a bias to be found throughout the volume. The author's thesis is: probation and parole work is social work, with law enforcement and other adaptations. It has borrowed much from the generic social work field. It has done some lending, too. Caseworkers have learned a great deal from probation and parole concerning the constructive meaning and use of authority, to cite one illustration.

Casework is a process seeking to bring about redirection of

[3] For interesting discussion on this, see T. C. Esselstyn, "Trends in Social Work toward Corrections," *Federal Probation*, XXI, No. 2 (1957), 30–33; and Ben S. Meeker, "Social Work and the Correctional Field," *Federal Probation*, XXI, No. 3 (1957), 32–42.

human behavior. That is why it is suited to the aims of the correctional field.

It will be a long time before the field is staffed completely, or almost completely, by trained social workers. Meantime, acceptable compromises must be made. Many workers trained in psychology, sociology, and other disciplines are performing effectively. There is no attempt to assert that *only* the trained social worker has made a contribution to the field. Rather, the argument is that, in recruiting from among thousands of candidates, the agency does best when it strikes out for professional social workers. It will thereby gain a small proportion who, by temperament, are unfit for the work, despite education in it. And it will lose a few who, though not educated in social work, would make splendid officers. But all in all, recruitment methods being crude at best, setting the standard of social work background should yield optimum results.

The Twofold Function

Probation and parole officers have a twofold function. The Federal Probation Officers Association has endorsed a statement on professional standards which includes this assertion: "The primary objective of probation and parole is the protection of society through the rehabilitation of the offender." [4] Here is the end result of the twofold function. The probation and parole officer is charged with a double responsibility: protecting society and aiding the offender. But there is no dichotomy here.

In the community protection role, these services have two obligations: to offer freedom and aid only to those not likely to assault society again; and to supervise them while treating them. Not every offender is fit for unrestricted liberty. Therefore, the court or parole board thinks first of community pro-

---

[4] "Professional Standards Endorsed by the Federal Probation Officers Association," *Federal Probation*, XXI, No. 1 (1957), 48.

tection in those cases; it will not turn an offender back to the community when he is an unsafe risk. As for those it does release, it will treat, but be constantly on guard against, potential recidivists.

But—and this is why social work treatment and law enforcement functions are not discrete elements—it will be noted we strive to help bring about social readjustment of offenders while remaining alert to signs of reversion to crime or delinquency. We protect society at the same time that we treat the offender. If we must choose at a given moment, we will accomplish the first by removing someone from the community. But fundamentally, the best community protection lies in so helping those who have offended that they no longer want to offend and no longer do violate the law. In this case, the twofold function brings one end result. In the sense of the statement of the Federal Probation Officers Association, protection of society is achieved through the rehabilitation of offenders.

Probation and parole, then, are casework services, in public agencies for the most part, that seek to select effectively from among offenders those who shall be offered the opportunities inherent in the programs. Practitioners of these services want to aid men and women, girls and boys, who need help in stabilizing themselves. They also try to assist and protect society and the probationer or parolee by bringing the two into mutual accommodation.

What, finally, are probation and parole? They are services designed to benefit society and the individual who is maladjusted in society. They are social work and law enforcement, not mutually exclusive and acting unilaterally, but cooperating and intertwined throughout.

If we agree that in most respects probation and parole are alike, we can from here on discuss them together. We shall do so in relation to etiological factors in crime and delinquency, investigation, and supervision in probation and parole agencies.

7

ETIOLOGICAL FACTORS IN
DELINQUENCY AND CRIME

Walter A. Lunden asked 453 college students, 200 prisoners, and 67 prison guards whether they believed people who commit our more serious crimes (murder, rape, etc.) have below average mentality.[1] Almost one fourth of the students thought so, as did one third of the prisoners and over 45 percent of the guards. About one third of each group also believed that insanity is a major cause of crime.

Since neither belief is borne out by facts, this response suggests the need for clarification on the etiology of delinquency and crime. Properly, such a discussion belongs in a criminology textbook, but since we must know something about what makes an offender in order that we may help him, some treatment of the subject is undertaken here.

What "causes" delinquency and crime? We know but little about this, yet every man is certain he has the answer. On crime, delinquency, international affairs, and politics, just about everyone considers himself an expert.

But surely there *are* experts who know what causes crime and delinquency? If so, they do not agree in their findings. Here, according to testimony given before legislative committees between 1954 and 1958 by presumed experts, are causes of delinquency: too much corporal punishment; not enough corporal

[1] Walter A. Lunden, *Prisons, Prisoners and People* (Ames, Iowa: Iowa State College, 1957; mimeographed), pp. 1–3.

punishment; underprivilege; overprivilege; too little familial affection; too much familial affection; absence of recreational facilities; too much leisure time; lack of education; overeducation; tough police; lenient police; feeble-mindedness; intellectual brilliance; neglectful parents; oversolicitous parents. Some authorities testified that comic books incited to delinquency; others, that they had no demonstrable effect upon children. A California Assembly subcommittee heard a Stanford University professor of law say that it is not known whether sex deviates become such through reading pornographic literature or whether they read the literature "because they have psychological problems." At the same hearing, a minister argued that "sex-mad magazines are creating criminals faster than jails can be built." [2]

Broken homes were adduced before investigative bodies as causal factors, while testimony to the contrary was also introduced. Use of narcotics or alcoholic beverages was advanced as a potent influence at the same time that other witnesses asserted they accounted for but little delinquency.

Other causes which had "yea" and "nay" advocates were: biological inferiority; modern advertising; pay-as you-go plans that divert a disproportionate share of the family income to keeping up with the neighbors; the doctrine of easy money; our materialistic culture; the credo of success; and the American cultural value of resistance to authority of any kind.[3]

The fact is, as we shall attempt to develop, that any one of the above factors *may* be influential in a *given* case, but none is a real "cause" of delinquency or crime.

[2] Marysville-Yuba City (Calif.) *Appeals-Democrat,* September 11, 1958.

[3] The sociologist Barron charges a "delinquent society" with producing offenders. An American value that appears significant in the etiology of delinquency, he suggests, is "toughness." While, he says, there is a social class distinction in this respect, in most strata of our society inordinate pressure is placed on boys, from their earliest years, to "fight back." They must not be "sissies." See Milton L. Barron, *The Juvenile in Delinquent Society* (New York: Alfred A. Knopf, 1954), p. 209.

What about statistics on causation? Certainly they tell us something? Yes. But they must be treated with the utmost caution. A numerical figure stuns us with its putative finality. There it is. Facts are facts. But are they? Artemus Ward once remarked that "It ain't so much the things we don't know that get us in trouble. It's the things we know that ain't so." [4]

Statistics "prove," according to J. Edgar Hoover, that our children are the most lawless in the history of the nation. "Proof" lies in the fact that there is more delinquency today than ever before. Yes? More delinquency or greater enforcement? More delinquency or readier identification of the delinquent? There might be scores of reasons to explain the statistical increase. Statistics "prove" that urban youth is more delinquent than rural. May it be that much rural delinquency remains unrecorded because it is treated informally? [5] Statistics on crime and delinquency are inadequate. Sometimes they actually traduce facts.

Causation

In seeking something solid on the subject of etiology, let us first understand the meaning of the word "cause." When one applies a certain amount of heat to a thermometer the indicator rises a precise number of degrees. It does so each and every time one does this. It is a safe assumption that heat is the cause of the temperature rise.

We have nothing like that in delinquency and crime. We do not have these phenomena each and every time we have a broken home or a child who reads a Dick Tracy comic book. We are aware of no factor which, when present, invariably produces conduct that society considers offensive. The most we

[4] Every reader owes it to himself to read the hilarious but solid treatment of this thesis in Darrell Huff, *How to Lie with Statistics* (New York: W. W. Norton Co., 1954).

[5] See Sophia M. Robison, *Can Delinquency Be Measured?* (New York: Columbia University Press, 1936).

can say is that a particular factor *seems* to play a significant part in the conduct of a *particular* case. We can only speak of general etiological factors that sometimes help produce the delinquent or criminal pattern.

Moreover, we know that almost never is one factor, whatever it be, responsible for criminality and delinquency. These phenomena are usually the end result of a group of interrelated factors. The sociologist Robert M. MacIver speaks of these as the interactive complex in causation.[6] There are not only pluralistic incentives to delinquency, he asserts, but the several factors make up a combination which is more than the sum of the parts. When a number of diverse factors are interactive, and when a given outcome derives from it, it is erroneous to treat the factors as though they were independent, each homogeneous unit producing a measurable portion of the joint product.

If we agree that there is no known cause of crime or delinquency, in that the factor, once present, always yields the phenomena; that no one factor in and of itself is likely to cause such conduct in a given case; and that such factors as are significant operate, not discretely and unilaterally, but in an interactive complex, then we may go a step further. We may study factors discretely, recognizing they are never discrete in a given situation.

Biological Influences

What part does heredity play in the etiology of delinquency and crime?

Followers of the Positive school of criminology saw the offender as a biological organism characteristically different from nonoffenders. In *L'uomo delinquente* (Criminal Man), published in 1876, Lombroso stated he had evidence of a born criminal, with atavistic characteristics marking him off from noncriminal individuals. This degenerate specimen deviated in

[6] Robert M. MacIver, *Social Causation* (Boston: Ginn, 1942), pp. 93–95.

size and shape of head from the type common to his race and region. His face was asymmetrical, jaw and cheek bones over-sized. His ears were either very large or small, and often stood out from his head, like a chimpanzee's. Among thieves, his nose was twisted, turned up, or flattened, while murderers had aquiline, beaklike proboscises. Hair anomalies and other features made the criminal man closer to the ape than to his law-abiding fellows.

Lombroso did not state flatly that every person born with physical stigmata was predestined to crime. He inclined rather to the proposition that such an individual was, by inheritance, predisposed to such behavior, and the more stigmata he possessed the greater the predisposition.

Later research has dispelled the notion that there is a "born" criminal type, predisposed to antisocial behavior. The offender has inherited no gene for criminality. For every criminal with a twisted nose and an underslung jaw there is likely to be a college professor or parole officer with like features. A man may inherit a nervous system or body structure which makes digging a ditch difficult for him, but he may resolve this difficulty by stealing for a living or by becoming a great pianist.

But the "born criminal" will not die, although he breathes with some discomfort today. The Harvard anthropologist Ernest A. Hooton had a variant of him.[7] And the German physiologist Johannes Lange thought he had established a relationship between heredity and crime in his study of identical twins.[8]

In a group of thirteen pairs of adult male monozygotic twins Lange found that where one member of a pair had a record of imprisonment, the other did too, in 77 percent of the cases. In a comparable group of seventeen pairs of fraternal twins,

[7] Ernest Albert Hooton, *Crime and the Man* (Cambridge, Mass.: Harvard University Press, 1939).

[8] Johannes Lange, *Verbrechen als schicksal: Studien an Kriminellen Zwillingen* (Leipzig: Geo. Thieme, 1929).

there was only 12 percent agreement in this respect. Doubt has been cast upon the validity of the Lange study, for it is uncertain that the so-called "identical" twins were indeed identical. Moreover, the influence of the environment was not eliminated as a factor in the study.

While European criminologists still lean toward neo-Lombrosian theory, students of the subject in this country are reasonably satisfied it lacks validity.

Another biological factor sometimes said to play a part in delinquency and criminality is physique, or body build. Is there a relation between physique and character? If people are born with body builds which give them a particular temperament, this could be a determinant in character formation, which in turn would be potent in directing behavior, criminal or otherwise. Artists, sensitive observers of the social scene, picture the genial gentleman as a short, plump, round-faced Mr. Pickwick, while the conniving, unhappy Uriah Heep is tall, attenuated, and aquiline of nose. What is the evidence?

Kretschmer, professor of psychiatry at the University of Tübingen, believes there is a high degree of correspondence between body type and temperament. The elongated asthenic type, for instance, is supposedly dour and pessimistic. On the basis of examination of over four thousand cases, Kretschmer holds there is a preponderance of the athletic type among persons committing crimes of violence. Individuals guilty of fraud and petty theft are disproportionately represented by the dour, elongated asthenic, while roly-poly pyknics lean to deception and fraud when they engage in crime. Dysplastics, who are mixed types, stand high in offenses against morality and decency.

Kretschmer theorizes further that one body type, the pyknic, is less given to crime generally than the athletic. However, he does not claim that criminal behavior is predestined by body type.

Sheldon, of Harvard, tends to support Kretschmer.[9] What he calls "endomorphs" (fat, soft, round) he believes have viscerotonic temperaments (relaxed, luxury-loving). "Mesomorphs" (muscular, heavy-chested) are somatonic (active, aggressive, dynamic). "Ectomorphs" (lean, fragile, delicate-boned) have a cerebrotonic temperament. (They are introverts, subject to functional disorders, skin eruptions, insomnia.) Sheldon ascribes characteristic behavior to each body type. But Vold points out:

In Sheldon's thinking the types are not to be considered as entities, but rather as degrees of interrelation, or tendency for one or the other pattern to be predominant. Each is therefore given a numerical value on a scale from one to seven, and the resultant type-descriptions, both physical and mental, take on numerical form instead of the customary wordy confusion of the usual psychiatric characterizations.[10]

By this device, Sheldon developed an index of delinquency, or "disappointingness." One young person might have a higher susceptibility to antisocial conduct than another because of predominance of one set of body characteristics over others.

Most recently, the cautious, meticulous researchers Sheldon and Eleanor T. Glueck have come out with a study tending to support the body-build theories, but with a number of qualifications.[11] More than previous investigators, they interrelate body build and social factors. Thus, while they found that mesomorphs were inclined toward delinquency, the Gluecks pointed to their relative extroversion and insensitivity which, in given situations, might render them more prone to attempt hazardous, aggressive physical adventures.

Kretschmer and others notwithstanding, the majority of stu-

[9] William H. Sheldon, *Varieties of Delinquent Youth* (New York: Harper, 1949).

[10] George B. Vold, *Theoretical Criminology* (New York: Oxford University Press, 1958), p. 71.

[11] Sheldon Glueck and Eleanor T. Glueck, *Physique and Delinquency* (New York: Harper, 1956).

dents in the field, at least in this country, hold that the evidence of the constitutional-theory researchers is incomplete or faulty.

What about intelligence? Is it correlated with delinquency and crime? For a time, it was widely held that feeble-mindedness predisposed to such behavior. The psychologist H. H. Goddard championed this thesis for years, conjecturing that at least 50 percent of all criminals were mental defectives. But as we learned more about what intelligence tests did and did not measure, and as we more carefully equated criminal and noncriminal samples, there appeared to be little or no difference. Earlier studies undoubtedly suffered from at least one serious shortcoming. They measured incarcerated offenders, found a higher percentage of feeble-mindedness than in the general population. Many circumstances suggest that defectives find their way into institutions more readily than do non-defectives.

Feeble-mindedness, per se, may conduce to delinquency and crime, given certain social conditions. But it also may not, given others. And in the offender population, as every probation and parole officer knows, will be found the subnormal, the average, and the superior. Nathan Leopold is in the gifted category; John Dillinger was not.

Is unlawful behavior precipitated by glandular dysfunction? Schlapp held it would not be surprising if it were found that a third of all convicts were suffering from emotional instability resulting from glandular or toxic disturbances.[12] Berman [13] studied 250 Sing Sing inmates, comparing them with a control group of noncriminal males. The former were found to have two to three times the glandular defects and disturbances of the latter.

[12] Max Gustav Schlapp, *The New Criminology: a Consideration of the Chemical Causation of Abnormal Behavior* (New York: Boni & Liveright, 1928).

[13] Louis Berman, *New Creations in Human Beings* (New York: Doubleday, Doran, 1938).

Research on this subject has brought considerable enlightenment to the study of personality, but much more work needs to be done. To date, there is no clear-cut case for a definite correlation between gland functioning and illegal conduct.

Can physical condition of the organism, whether involving glands or not, produce delinquency and crime? It can, but we do not know to what extent this is a significant factor.

A very interesting example of the relation between physical condition and behavior in a given case is that of a man, walking along the street, who suddenly broke into a gallop, raced into a candy store, violently shoved the proprietor aside, and seized a handful of candy bars, with which he ran out. Technically, he had committed a crime.

His case illustrates the occasional relationship, in the individual instance, between sugar metabolism and crime. An abnormal drop in body sugar produces hypoglycemia, with its dramatic symptoms. The autonomic indicators in such cases include perspiration, hand tremors, rise or drop in pulse rate and blood pressure. Corresponding mental changes are weakness of concentration, difficulty in decision-making, extreme anxiety, depression, and irritability. The body craves sugar, and the man we described was driven to desperate means to secure it without delay.

Now this condition need not lead to unlawful acts, and it does not often do so, although, as we have seen, it can. It is not alone a desperate demand for sugar that might result in conduct defined as antisocial. Irritability produced by hypoglycemia may produce other eruptive, violent behavior. We have all read about mothers who kill their own babies. Asked why, they try to explain something they actually do not understand. They say, "I couldn't stand his crying"; or, "He just wouldn't go to sleep. He was driving me crazy!" Doctors know that a significant number of such tragedies occur shortly after childbirth, when the mother's body sugar has taken a marked drop. Feeding the body the sugar it requires restores emotional and physical equilibrium.

Dr. Joseph Wilder compiled a list of crimes committed under the influence of insulin or in a state of spontaneous hypoglycemia. It included disorderly conduct, assault, homicide, cruelty against children or spouse, sexual deviations and aggressions, embezzlement, petty larceny, arson, and others.[14]

But we emphasize again that while it is possible to determine a fairly direct relationship between a physical condition and antisocial behavior in individual cases, we do not know how statistically significant the factor may be generally.

Environmental Influences

If biology offers no single factor which inevitably produces antisocial conduct or which can be shown to have a measurable effect in general, what about man's environment?

One of the most popular and persistent of theories is that economic status is a highly significant factor. Common sense suggests this must be so. Let us examine the evidence.

In 1883, in a floor discussion at the annual meeting of the National Conference of Charities and Correction, a Mr. Vaux advanced the premise that poverty produced domestic discord, and discord engendered crime. When a man comes home to a hungry family, "and his wife meets him with upbraidings made bitter by the situation, what can he do?" Mr. Vaux asked. "You cannot undertake to do with her as you do with a man. You must treat her in a certain way. She becomes violent. Where does he go? Some other place than such a home, for that pity and comfort that he should receive at home, and in such a case he is ready to do anything. Is not this an element in crime-cause?"

[14] Joseph Wilder, "Sugar Metabolism in Its Relation to Criminology," in Robert M. Lindner and Robert V. Seliger, eds., *Handbook of Correctional Psychology* (New York: Philosophical Library, 1947), pp. 98–129.

A Mrs. Spencer hotly protested that the remarks calumniated her sex. The minutes report: "The Conference then took a recess till afternoon." [15]

Mrs. Spencer notwithstanding, study suggests that loss of status within the family occasioned by the wage earner's inability to provide may be *a* factor in domestic discord. This does not imply it is *the* factor which is almost certain to spell crime.

Hundreds of studies have been published here and abroad on the subject of economic condition and criminality. They are surprisingly lacking in agreement, and often faulty in methodology.

Bonger reported a number of comparisons of price indexes and crime rate, made by himself and others. The technique was simple in one. Chart the price of potatoes. Superimpose a curve for crime rate. Bonger found that as prices rose the crime rate did, too. He concluded that the part played by economic conditions was preponderant, even decisive.[16]

Burt eschewed the effect of the potato on crime and studied 113 English prostitutes, finding that some 7 percent came from poor homes while 30 percent came from comfortable families.[17] Inferentially, this delivers a fillip to the nose of Monsieur Bonger.

Wiers made a comparison, for the years 1921–43, between fluctuations in juvenile delinquency court cases and certain indexes of economic conditions in Wayne County, Michigan. He found delinquency high in good times.[18] But Poletti con-

[15] *Proceedings of the Tenth Annual National Conference of Charities and Correction, 1883*, pp. 202–4.

[16] William A. Bonger, *Criminality and Economic Conditions* (Boston: Little, Brown, 1916).

[17] Cyril Burt, "Cause of Sex Delinquency in Girls," *Health and Empire*, No. 1 (1926), pp. 251–71; reviewed in Jerome Michael and Mortimer J. Adler, *Crime, Law and Social Science* (New York: Harcourt, Brace & Co., 1933), p. 125.

[18] Paul Wiers, "Wartime Increase in Michigan Delinquency," *American Sociological Review*, X (1945), 515–23.

cluded from *his* study that with good times crime declines.[19]

One of the more careful studies, by Thomas, investigated the relationship between the business cycle and crime in England, 1857–1913. Some of the findings were: There was no close correlation between the trend of all indictable offenses and offenses against property without violence, and the business cycle. Offenses against property with violence increased in times of depression. There was little connection between the business cycle and crimes against the person.[20]

But Woytinsky challenged these findings. He discovered a high positive correlation between the business cycle and crimes against property with violence.[21]

And to compound confusion, Wagner held there was no positive correlation at all between business cycle, depressions, and crime arrests.[22]

You may take your choice. As Vold points out:

. . . assumptions involving either *positive* or *negative* relationships with economic conditions may be supported with some show of statistical significance. The obvious inference is that the general relations of economic conditions and criminality are so indefinite that no clear or definite conclusion can be drawn. Hence there is a general tendency to accept the position that economic conditions represent only one of a large number of environmental circumstances. As such, this then becomes part of the "multiple factor" approach to causation.[23]

Do broken homes contribute to delinquency and crime? We have been saying so for years. More recently we have taken a second look.

[19] Reported in Vold, *op. cit.*, pp. 174–75.
[20] Dorothy Swain Thomas, *Social Aspects of the Business Cycle* (New York: Alfred A. Knopf, 1927).
[21] W. Woytinsky, "Kriminalitat und Lebensmittelpreise," *Zeitschrift dur die gesamte Strafrechtswissenschaft*, XLIX (1929), 647–75.
[22] Albert C. Wagner "Crime and Economic Change in Philadelphia, 1925–1934," *Journal of Criminal Law and Criminology*, XXVII (1936), 483–90.
[23] Vold, *op. cit.*, pp. 181–82.

Studies of inmate populations almost always show a higher proportion of individuals from broken homes than is found in the population at large. But an institutional sampling is not valid. The child from a broken home is more likely to be entered into an institution than is one who can be returned to his parents after a court appearance. Other considerations which vitiate our earlier beliefs about the importance of broken homes as a factor are these: They do not, of course, in and of themselves produce antisocial behavior, however heavily the factor may weigh in a specific case. The individual's age when the home was broken may be a variable, and we have not given this enough attention. There may be differences in impact by sex. And the breakup of a home, far from producing tensions, sometimes creates a healthier atmosphere, as when death, divorce, or separation removes the adult largely responsible for the tensions. A broken home is not necessarily an unhappy one.

Nye's study supports the hypothesis that too much may have been made of broken homes. He investigated unreported delinquency, a novel approach. His subjects were school children who had not been formally adjudicated delinquents. They did not have an institutional experience. They admitted anonymously that they had committed acts which would be defined as delinquent if known. His findings included:

. . . less delinquent behavior was found in broken homes than in unhappy unbroken homes. The *happiness* of the marriage was found to be much more closely related to delinquent behavior in children than whether the marriage was an original marriage or a remarriage or one in which the child was living with one parent only.[24]

Religious training is surely a factor highly correlated with conduct? It is impossible to study the relationship, because no one can satisfactorily define a religious person for research

[24] F. Ivan Nye, *Family Relationships and Delinquent Behavior* (New York: John Wiley & Sons, 1958), p. 51.

purposes. What is your religion? You will answer "Protestant," "Catholic," "Jewish," or other, perhaps because your parents called themselves that. You are nominally of that faith. But do you have *faith*? Do you practice what your church preaches?

Logically, the truly religious person, except possibly a compulsive offender, would not commit crime; for every major religion, in one way or another, preaches the Golden Rule. We could argue that the very fact an individual committed a crime means he was not religious. You can see how easily we would get into semantics and a philosophical Donnybrook, pursuing such a course.

But suppose we use as an index, invalid as it may be, the fact of church affiliation. This would be in deference to the thousands of judges and probation and parole officers, who at one time or another have prescribed church attendance as an antidote to undesirable behavior.

Other factors held constant (if possible), does attendance at church and Sunday school decrease susceptibility to delinquency and crime? Unfortunately, there is little solace for those who would so insist.

Hartshorne and May found no meaningful difference in honesty between children attending Sunday school and those not attending.[25] Reform school boys and girls, according to other studies, had received about the same religious training in church and Sunday school as had nondelinquent children. Several researchers found an interesting phenomenon among both delinquents and nondelinquents. The stricter parents were about church and Sunday school attendance, the more likely the children were to be emotionally maladjusted and/or delinquent.

Clearly, both church-affiliated and nonaffiliated children commit delinquencies. Even if statistical analysis were to re-

[25] H. Hartshorne and M. A. May, *Studies in the Nature of Character*, 3 vols. (New York: Macmillan, 1928–30).

veal that the rate for the nonaffiliated is greater than for the affiliated, we have no ground for saying that affiliation is the determining variable unless we are able to control all other variables, and we have not done so to date.

Education? Is it a demonstrable factor? No evidence exists to support the thesis that the better educated individual is less likely to get into trouble than the relatively uneducated.

Slums? Delinquency areas? Governors and gunmen have come from such sections. And some of the worst neighborhoods produce little delinquency and crime. In Baltimore, for instance, it was found that several low-rent areas, with great overcrowding, did not fall in even the upper 25 percent of ranking delinquency areas.[26]

Culture conflict between old and new generation? This has, in individual cases, been one of a number of factors seemingly responsible for a delinquent or criminal pattern. But again, the relative importance of the factor is unknown.

Emotional Factors

Do emotional factors produce antisocial behavior? There are all kinds of evidence that they do, but not that a given emotional state inevitably results in such phenomena.

Insanity is an emotional state, but we may rule it out of consideration in this discussion of etiology, since in the eyes of the law a psychotic person cannot commit crime.[27]

Other emotional states indirectly result in crime, particularly where frustration is present. Frustration leads to various characteristic reactions, one of them aggression. And aggression is sometimes of a sort that we define as "criminal." One psychiatrist, with extensive experience in treating the delinquent-criminal group, writes:

[26] Harold L. Wilensky and Charles N. Lebeaux, *Industrial Society and Social Welfare* (New York: Russell Sage Foundation, 1958), p. 185.

[27] Medical and legal insanity are not the same, of course, but that is another subject.

Aggression is commonly described as a product of frustration; and all crime, petty or large, is a form of aggression. The relatively normal person is subject to the same frustrations, but he accepts them as a challenge and overcomes them, or at least accepts them by adjusting his situation to the matrix of reality. Some emotionally unstable persons, lacking this flexibility, when confronted by frustration discharge their aggression violently, as a child does, by attacking the denying force either directly or through some substitute channel.[28]

Then at last we have the differential in delinquency and crime? No, for as Banay indicates, the relatively normal person acts one way about frustration; the unstable, another. And two emotionally unstable people will behave differently about somewhat the same kind of frustration.

We have, then, still to determine what makes one unhappily married man shoot his wife, while a second man deserts his, a third surrenders to her, and a fourth escapes into schizophrenia.

Causation and Motivation

If we know little about etiology generally, this is not so true where causation in an individual case is concerned. We cannot, in the present state of knowledge, speak authoritatively about factors known to be highly significant in producing offenders. The best we can do is to study the individual offender, examine into the many factors that may have contributed to *his* pattern of behavior. We go a step further and try to understand his motivation. For instance: two men are unhappily wed. One commits a crime in order to escape his wife; that is, he murders her. The other begins to treat his mate much better than theretofore, and the friction diminishes. Each had the same factor in his background; it played some

[28] Ralph S. Banay, *We Call Them Criminals* (New York: Appleton-Century-Crofts, 1957), p. 6.

part in the resulting behavior. Each was differently motivated in seeking a solution to his problem.

An investigation of motivation, while it will not tell us the general causal factors in crime and delinquency, can throw some light upon what made a given individual behave as he did in given circumstances.

The meaning of an unlawful act is never quite the same in any two cases. Hence we must individualize each offender, attempt to uncover, from study of his background, what made this man act this way this time. Thus we glean clues to appropriate treatment.

However, the fact that a person committed an act under given motivation does not mean he is still so motivated. The factors that produced the disapproved conduct may no longer play a part in the life organization of the individual, and we should not assume they necessarily must be considered in planning treatment. To use the unhappy husband example again, the man who murdered his wife no longer has a wife who so upsets him as to lead to homicide.

In theory, by the time a probationer or parolee comes under supervision, he and his circumstances are already somewhat changed. The question is in what direction he is motivated today, how he meets his problems currently. At this stage it may serve little purpose to attempt to deduce the present from the past. In fact, it is sometimes easier to deduce the past from observation of the present. It cannot be assumed that because a criminal pattern once existed it necessarily exists today, although this is frequently the case. And it cannot be subsumed that if the impulse to crime or delinquency remains alive during the probation or parole period, as frequently happens, the clue to a remedy lies solely and exclusively in the past. Every man has been, is, and is in the process of becoming.

8

INVESTIGATION IN
PROBATION AND PAROLE

The first step in the probation or parole process is selection. It is a crucial matter. Poor selection can render supervision and treatment ineffective and can jeopardize the community as well. Human nature being what it is, the mind fallible, and our ability to forecast behavior limited, there will always be some errors of judgment. We cannot predict recidivism with complete efficiency. But we can apply the soundest selective methods known.

Intake

In a casework agency, when an applicant comes voluntarily for some service, he is usually first seen by an intake worker who interviews him to determine as quickly and as painlessly as possible whether this is the agency that can best meet his needs. In a very real sense, selection for probation and parole is intake, too. The judge and parole board are in the position of intake workers. Upon their evaluations will depend the nature and quality of caseloads. If their policies are sound, they will choose those individuals who can profit from treatment. The more refined the selective processes, the less probation and parole officers will have to engage in law enforcement activities. Judge and parole authority, then, are strategic factors in the total social work program.

Probation Selection

It is a judge who, in the first instance, undertakes to make a diagnostic study of the offender before him. He will be aided in this by a probation investigation report. He asks himself, "What is the best treatment, in the interest of society and offender? Shall this defendant be incarcerated or placed on probation?" He operates on the theory that probation is not for all offenders, but only for certain of them.

It is generally accepted that probation should be extended to those who offer considerable hope of readjustment. It is, by consensus, for those least hardened in crime, for individuals willing and anxious to accept probation conditions as an alternative to incarceration.

Ideally, selection is based upon individualization of offenders. There are no blanket rules. Some older men are better risks than adolescents, and vice versa. Some repeaters may have reached that psychological milepost which marks an inclination to become law-abiding, whereas a particular first offender may be a very poor risk in this regard. One gunman may be a hazard while another gunman is deserving of a chance on probation.

Some judges have suggested that at least with juveniles the bench follow five mandates basic to the disposition of delinquency cases:

1. Individualize the child.

2. Have an awareness of how the child views himself.

3. Weigh the past in terms of the future.

4. Do not tie your hands with clichés like, "Probation is for first offenders only," or, "Only one chance on probation."

5. Determine the type and quality of treatment services available and select what is needed.[1]

[1] *Guides for Juvenile Court Judges,* prepared by the Advisory Council of Judges of the National Probation and Parole Association, in cooperation with the National Council of Juvenile Court Judges (New York: National Probation and Parole Association, 1957), paraphrased from pp. 70–82.

All five mandates are actually encompassed in the first. The judge knows that if maximum efficiency is to be achieved, each case will have to be studied individually. Here, the probation department can be most helpful. The better its investigation reports, the more useful they can be to the conscientious jurist.

The probation report serves a number of purposes. It helps the court arrive at an appropriate adjudication. If the defendant is placed on probation, the report is a starting point for supervision. Should the offender be incarcerated, the investigation material serves as background toward formulation of a program for the inmate which will make it possible for him to get the maximum usefulness out of his term. Presumably, too, the report will be utilized by the parole board when the prisoner is eligible for release, part of it being incorporated into the preparole investigation.

The judge studies the report and asks himself:

1. Is the offender dangerous at the present time?

2. Will incarceration help or harm him?

3. Is probation an acceptable, constructive substitute for institutionalization in this particular individual's case?

4. Is he mentally and emotionally capable of profiting from probation treatment?

5. Is his attitude toward society and probation such as to justify the use of probation in lieu of incarceration?

6. Will society, in the long run, benefit if the defendant is placed on probation? Will the individual benefit?

7. Will granting probation at this time be construed by the offender as leniency, that he is "beating the rap," and thus be deleterious rather than helpful?

How can a probation report answer such questions? By going into depth as much as possible. By presenting rounded, full pictures of individuals. By showing as realistically as possible what the defendant is like, how he got that way, where he thinks he is going, and how he interacts in his environment to satisfy his objectives.

No outline or instructions will guarantee that sort of report. Its quality will depend upon the skill, imagination, understanding, and intelligence of the officer who prepares it. It will cover at least these pertinent areas:

1. *Details of the present offense.*—Where and when was it committed? Under what circumstances? What was the *modus operandi?* If more than one person participated, who planned it? Who was the leader? What part did this defendant play? Was he armed? Sober? Seemingly sane at the time? Compulsive? Hysterical? Calm?

Why, you may ask, is all this necessary? Do not these facts come out in court? Not necessarily. Where a juvenile is concerned there is, of course, no formal trial. With an adult, there will be none if the defendant pleads guilty. And when a trial is conducted, not all the facts are introduced as evidence. Yet those omitted may be extremely valuable as diagnostic material. Consider these two cases:

A cab driver found a wallet, left in the vehicle by a fare. It contained almost a thousand dollars. The driver was in financial straits due to the fact his wife had had a series of costly operations. Tempted, he kept the wallet instead of turning it in. Eventually, he was arrested and convicted.

A woman of means was found to have stolen expensive jewelry and other items from guests in her own home. The cold record showed she was subsequently charged with grand larceny. But she was a compulsive thief (sometimes called a "kleptomaniac"). Her closets were crammed with odds and ends, some valueless, all purloined.

Was there not a great difference, in treatment needs, between one case and the other?

Other questions regarding an offense belong in a report:

Did the offender admit his guilt upon arrest? What is his attitude toward his participation in the offense? Does he show remorse, anger, ill will? What seem to be his feelings toward the victim? Toward the police? How much loss or personal injury resulted from the offense?

2. *Previous criminal or delinquency history.*—How extensive is it? What may it signify? Does it have a characteristic pattern of offense? Does the record suggest we are dealing with an amateur, a compulsive, or a professional offender?

3. *Codefendants.*—Were there such? What was the role of each? What disposition, if any, was made of their cases?

4. *Attitude of the complainant.*—The court will want to consider the complainant's attitude, particularly in instances where he has been physically injured or has lost a considerable amount of property to the offender. The judge will not necessarily act according to the wishes of the injured person, yet he will want to have that individual's attitude defined in the report.

5. *Personal history.*—Meat and bone of the probation report is the social history of the offender—his birth, developmental history where significant, health, education, employment record, personal habits, character, personality, associates, recreation, marital life, mental condition, intellectual status, interrelationships. How did he interact within his family as a child? As an adult? How did he get along with people generally? What unusual illnesses, trauma, accidents, or other events may have conditioned him? In what ways?

Every meaningful item the probation officer discovers goes toward the production of the report, so that the subject may emerge as an understandable human being.

6. *Family history and relationships.*—The family is the offender's primary group, and the one which was probably most influential in his socialization. The court needs data on the parents, siblings, wife, children, and paramours of the defend-

ant. Who are they? How old? What sort of personality does each possess? What was the impact of that person upon the offender? What are the attitudes of these people toward the defendant at this time?

7. *Community conditions.*—From what sort of environment does the offender come? How do members of the community feel toward him at this time? Is there great hostility in the area for the defendant? Sympathy? Indifference? Is it likely, were he returned to the community at once, that he would be received without animus?

8. *Probation program.*—Should the court wish to invoke probation, where would the defendant live? Where would he work? Under what conditions? Has the offender himself done anything toward setting up this prospective program?

Parole Selection

In carrying out the intake policy of parole, the paroling authority is the counterpart of the judge who makes the selection in the probation process. It asks itself much the same questions as would a jurist:

1. Is the inmate a fit risk for parole?

2. Will he be able to profit from treatment, or is he likely to recidivate?

3. Does he have a favorable attitude toward society, so far as can be determined?

4. Does he want parole?

5. If the board grants parole, will the prisoner agree to abide by rules and regulations?

In arriving at answers to these and other questions bearing on the question of possible release, parole boards use four aids, singly or in combination: the preparole investigation; institutional reports; prediction tables; and the personal interview with the inmate. No jurisdiction uses prediction tables exclusively; some do not have a preparole investigation made in the field; while others dispense with the personal interview. All four aids, however, when employed, may be considered part of the investigation process in parole.

A good preparole report, based upon field investigation, would appear to be an essential, whether or not other aids are utilized. This case history is much like a probation investigation in subject matter, though some differences are possible.

Many parole authorities seek to determine the attitude of the sentencing or adjudicating judge toward release. The district attorney may also be consulted when adult offenders are involved. Often his comment is well worth consideration; sometimes it is so perfunctory as to be useless. One district attorney for years made an identical recommendation in every case: "I am opposed to parole in the premises." His signature, appropriately, was by rubber stamp.

Particularly when the inmate would, if released, return to a small community where anonymity is impossible, parole authorities attempt to gauge public sentiment toward the prospective parolee. This is in the interest of both community and inmate. If the ex-prisoner returns to a community which meets him with hostility, he may aggress against it again, to the detriment both of the parolee and of his victims. It might, in such a prospect, be more practical to allow the inmate to make a more hopeful start in another area.[2]

In both probation and parole, the person under consideration must have a satisfactory home and employment program, if he is an adult, and at least a home if he is a juvenile. But the prisoner has had a greater separation from home than has the defendant being considered for probation. Is there still family available to receive the inmate? If not, can he safely be housed in a residence club? A furnished room? Is a change

[2] The judge, in considering probation for a defendant, is also interested in gauging public opinion. But he frequently does not have to make close inquiry. Members of the community and representative groups often express their views without solicitation, to him and in the press.

of locale proposed by the prisoner? Does this mean that an urbanite would be transplanted to rural territory or vice versa? If so, what is the outlook? Furthermore, the inmate's work in the institution has not been performed under the competitive conditions he will encounter on the outside. He may have lost his speed, skills, or both. The preparole investigation will pay attention to these matters in reporting parole program.

Is the job offer bonafide? Is the work of the sort the parolee can do? Does it offer adequate income? Under the same conditions as those applied to nonparolees?

Indications are that a stable home environment is of the utmost value in giving a parolee a start back to responsible living in free society. Research further emphasizes that, with adults particularly, a job upon release is a positive element in readjustment.

In this connection, there are interesting data to be found in the Attorney General's *Survey of Release Procedures*. Of 34,-674 parolees employed at the time of original arrest, 23 percent violated parole, while of 25,379 not so employed, 36 percent became parole violators. And of 7,663 parolees unemployed throughout their parole period, 53 percent became parole violators, while of 22,753 who were working during the parole period, only 17 percent violated the terms of their parole. Still further, offenders unemployed all the time they were on parole were more likely to violate by a new offense while under supervision than offenders who were employed throughout the parole period. Moreover, partially employed parolees were more likely to succeed on parole than those who were altogether unemployed, and less likely to finish parole satisfactorily than parolees employed full time. The *Survey* comments: "On the whole the results of the analyses . . . on employment indicate that the emphasis placed upon employment by paroling authorities is entirely warranted." [3]

[3] United States Attorney General, *Survey of Release Procedures* (Washington, D.C.: U.S. Department of Justice, 1939), II, 455.

More recent research sustains these findings. Ohlin determined that the category "inadequate parole job" in the prediction tables used in Illinois had the highest violation rate of any single-factor prediction category used for adult offenders.[4]

The inmate under consideration for parole has had an institutional experience. Therefore, institution reports are a source of evaluative data. Good physical, psychometric, and psychiatric reports are of great value. Unfortunately, one of the most glaring deficiencies of our correctional institutions is the paucity of medical, psychological, and psychiatric service, particularly the last.

Other institutional reports can answer questions such as: How has the inmate made use of his time? Has he studied? Learned a trade? Been industrious? Ambitious? Is he better prepared to earn a living? How has he used leisure time? With what sort of inmates did he customarily associate, by choice? Was he a leader or a follower? Generally outgoing or reserved? Did he show a social sense in matters requiring group cooperation?

Not many institutions are prepared to go as deeply into such matters as indicated. Where it is done, the results are gratifyingly valuable for parole bodies. In New York's Wallkill State Prison, for instance, personnel at all levels are trained to note and record such items in a central file kept in the Service Unit. The parole board has found this most useful. The institution is a laboratory for observing inmates under all sorts of conditions, studying their reactions and interactions, their personalities and motivations. We need to make greater use of this opportunity for studying men, women, and children who will be future parolees.

Still other data can, in most instances, be furnished by in-

[4] Lloyd E. Ohlin, *Selection for Parole: a Manual for Parole Prediction* (New York: Russell Sage Foundation, 1951).

stitutions: With whom did the inmate correspond? Who visited him? These often constitute leads to the ties the inmate has retained, the people with whom he will make contact upon release.

Perhaps the most germane question is: What is the inmate's present attitude toward society, crime (or delinquency), his relations to others, his obligations to his fellow men? The mental attitude of the prisoner is of vital concern to the releasing body. Comparatively few institutions are equipped to analyze and report upon this. The busy warden or superintendent is likely to characterize the inmate's attitude as satisfactory if he has not been outstandingly rebellious. The psychiatrist (if any) may report on the basis of one interview, which probably took place upon reception of the inmate. The chaplain is perhaps favorably impressed if the prisoner, sincerely or shrewdly, attended religious services. Custodial officers possibly consider the truckling inmate an individual with a highly satisfactory attitude. And so on.

And if the reports be adequate, they often suffer from lack of integration. The dentist knows John Doe as a set of teeth; the doctor, as a liver and spleen he once probed; the psychologist, as an I.Q.; the vocational director, as an automaton who oils machinery; and the disciplinarian, as the person who stole a bun from the kitchen. In many institutions little attempt is made to put teeth, liver, spleen, mind, vocation, and morals together and make of them John Doe, human being.

The inadequacies implicit in such segmentation of the individual are suggested by the following case:

Morris, at 19, was sentenced to an industrial institution of the reformatory type. When he appeared before the parole board it noted, from institutional reports, that:

He had an unusually good presentence history, having been arrested (and acquitted) only once before the present offense.

He was of average intelligence and seemingly of sound mind. (There was no psychiatrist practicing in the institution.)

He had had three years of high school, and was presumed to be skilled in mechanics. He was assigned to the reformatory's machine shop for training.

His conduct in the institution had been atrocious. In the one year he spent in custody he had been reported no fewer than forty times for misconduct. The record revealed, with shocking regularity, punishment for insolence to officers and refusal to work.

The parole board member reading the case folder realized that despite the many favorable indicators, Morris could not be paroled, for to do so would create a discipline problem in the institution. If he "got away with it," other inmates would be the more ready to flout regulations.

Considering this important administrative matter, the board member flipped a page in the file and came upon the physician's report. It showed but one examination, made upon reception of the inmate. It noted that Morris had a serious orthopedic condition which made standing even for ten minutes at a stretch excruciating. The physician recommended immediate surgery.

But his report got filed along with all the others prepared at the point of reception of Morris, and nothing was done to carry out the recommendation. Nobody related the medical report to any of the subsequent institutional history of the prisoner.

It was reasonable to assume that at least part of Morris's insolence to officers and refusal to work stemmed from irascibility born of pain induced by standing before a machine four hours at a time.

The parole board called the doctor's report to the attention of the superintendent. Morris received surgical treatment. His conduct became exemplary, so that he could be paroled six months after emerging from the hospital.

One of the finest examples of the reverse of this situation, of thoroughgoing integration of all data, is to be found in New York's Wallkill State Prison. When Dr. Walter M. Wallack became warden, he reexamined the Service Unit, which had been operated cooperatively by the institution and the parole board. He eliminated its organizational defects, gave it new direction, and made the unit useful. One central file for each prisoner was set up in the Service Unit. No matter which staff member has contact with the inmate, when, or how often, those contacts are recorded in the one file in chronological sequence. In one place, then, can be found results of medical examinations, chaplains' reports, progress statements by the educational and vocational director, observations of guards concerning yard behavior and associates, reports of other custodial officers on the inmate's demeanor in the visiting room —everything that happens to a prisoner is there.

These data are not filed and forgotten. Members of the Service Unit review them regularly. If an inmate is not showing interest or progress in a vocational training assignment, he is interviewed to determine why: Does he want a change of assignment? Can he think of a more suitable vocation for himself? If the prisoner has been losing time for misconduct, the Service Unit wants to know the underlying reasons.

From Dr. Wallack to the guard, the door is open to prisoners who wish to discuss their problems. By the time an inmate is eligible for parole, the Service Unit has a picture of him as a *personality*. The imagination and creativity of the warden made this possible, and the parole board takes his recommendations on inmates very seriously.

California has developed what is probably the most consistent and thoroughgoing evaluative program of any state-level correctional system. Under Director of Corrections Richard A. McGee and with the advisory aid of the Adult Authority, all adult inmates, upon admission, are held in a reception-guidance center where they are put through extensive examination, testing, and interviewing. The center's records follow the inmate to the institution where he will serve his time. Here cumulative records are kept, progress (or lack of it) watched, and appropriate changes made in the prisoner's program where this is indicated.

The earnestness with which the Director of Corrections regards the principle of individualization of offenders is demonstrated by the comparatively high ratio of professional staff to inmates. Here again is an illustration of the fact that creative leadership is the factor that makes prisons and reformatories as effective as it is possible for them to be, considering that the environment provided by such institutions is at best abnormal.

We turn now to the third aid in selection for parole: prediction tables.[5] These are, in a sense, actuarial tables which compute the statistical chance that a given individual will remain at large without violating his parole or breaking the law. The first such instrument was formulated by Bruce, Burgess, Harno, and Landesco.[6] They studied a thousand cases in Illinois prisons, analyzing various factors present in those men who were paroled and relating these to outcome while under supervision. Thus, if 80 percent of the cases had factor A in their backgrounds and succeeded, while 20 percent had the same factor but failed, an inmate with factor A was deemed, with regard to that factor alone, to have an 80 percent chance of succeeding on parole. The assumption was that there was a definite relationship between the number of favorable factors and parole success.

There are a number of other prediction tables, including those compiled by Sheldon and Eleanor T. Glueck, Elio Monachesi, G. B. Vold, and C. Tibbits.

Are prediction tables a useful tool? There is indication that they are. Parole violations dropped to a low of 26 percent from a high of 57 percent when a predictive instrument came into use in Illinois. Of course, were we to attribute the decline to the use of the tables exclusively, ignoring other possible influences, we might be guilty of the *post hoc ergo propter hoc* fallacy. But we need not adopt an all-or-nothing position. There still

[5] For what they are worth—and that is considerable—it is a matter of some wonder that probation has made practically no use of these tables. If they are useful to a degree for parole, should they not be so for probation?

[6] Andrew A. Bruce, Ernest W. Burgess, Albert J. Harno, and John Landesco, "A Study of the Indeterminate Sentence and Parole in the State of Illinois," *Journal of the American Institute of Criminal Law and Criminology*, XIX, No. 1, Part 2 (1928), 5–306.

seems to be evidence that prediction tables are at least fairly efficient prognostic aids. A criminologist asserts that, without contesting the value of case-history information in making selection for parole, "it does seem to be true that an actuarial method . . . is more efficient . . . than is a prognostic method based on the judgment of board members who are looking into the merits of each case." [7]

There is general agreement that prediction tables should not at present be depended upon as the sole selection device. They "are not intended to replace men with a fund of knowledge and experience in making selection for parole release. They are intended rather to serve such men in making decisions." [8]

Prediction tables may someday replace the human judgments of parole board members, but if this is to be so, the tables will need to be refined. They all suffer from certain weaknesses:

It is difficult, and sometimes impossible, to determine whether a given factor exists in a person's background. Certain highly important items, such as an inmate's attitudes on particular subjects, may be impossible to gauge. How is it to be ascertained beyond reasonable doubt whether an inmate really wants to be law-abiding on the outside? How are we to know whether he really has forgiven his wife's infidelity, as he says, or intends to take revenge the day he is paroled?

Some factors are fortuitous. Possession of a weapon in the commission of a robbery might be scored as a negative item, decreasing the owner's statistical chance of nonrecidivism. Yet the individual concerned might not have had a gun because he had his codefendant hold it at the last moment. Or he might have had one because his codefendant gave it to *him* a moment before the robbery.

But the greatest shortcoming appears to be that while the tables rate past and present, they cannot hope to do much

[7] Walter C. Reckless, *The Crime Problem* (New York: Appleton-Century-Crofts, 1955), p. 639.

[8] Alfred C. Schnur, "Predicting Parole Outcome," *Focus*, XXVIII (1949), 70.

about rating the immediate future. What measurement device can evaluate such intangibles as the effect it may produce upon the newly released parolee if he finds his job offer is not bona-fide? Who can place a plus or minus value on the personality of the parole officer who will take the released man's arrival report? Who can measure the effect upon a particular man of discovering that his wife intends to divorce him, but had not told him so while he was incarcerated? Suppose the parolee finds himself in a personality clash with his supervising officer? Suppose he discovers his children want nothing to do with him? We have not yet found a way of predicting the possibilities of such eventualities or surmising the part they will play in recidivism or nonrecidivism.

It will probably be a long time before prediction tables meet with complete acceptance by parole authorities, particularly if it is contemplated that they replace the personal interview with the inmate eligible for parole. To the experienced, intelligent board member with *simpatico* and sufficient objectivity the personal interview can reveal much, provided certain hazards are taken into account.

The inmate's reactions before a parole board supplement the impressions gained from the written reports. On paper, a prisoner may seem an excellent risk, while in person he dispels that impression. Or vice versa. Which shall we believe?

The inmate may create a better impression than is justified. He may deliberately strive to create an unrealistic view of himself. The hearing will decide his fate. He would be less than human if he did not sometimes attempt to delude the men who sit in judgment. Some prisoners appear contrite, even truckling, when in fact they feel little contrition and are inwardly trucu-lent. They castigate themselves, maintaining, "I've got no one to blame but myself." They weep. If more astute, they may put on a convincing display of self-respect and inner strength, fight-ing back the tears and asking for no quarter. Often these displays, both lachrymose and reserved, are genuine. Just as often, they are not. The hazard lies in selecting one interpretation or the other.

Then, too, the inmate may create a worse impression than is justified. He comes in, tense, nervous, excited. As a result, he may be so taciturn as to lead to the inference that he is withholding his true feelings. On the other hand, tension may provoke an explosion in which he angrily berates his listeners, says things he scarcely means. The author has heard many inmates vehemently declare they care not a continental whether they be paroled or not, when every indication was that, in their more relaxed and lucid moments, they would fervently ask for the opportunity to start life anew on the outside.

A serious shortcoming connected with the personal appearance is the necessary brevity of the interviews. It conditions both prisoner and board member. It is impossible, in five, ten, or fifteen minutes, to cover the ground that ought to be covered. The inmate feels frustrated because he cannot take time to relax to the point where he can say what he wants and mean what he says. The board member must get to the next case. In his hurry, he will often not allow himself the time he knows he needs if he is to examine all relevant facets of the case.

No doubt a personal interview can be an aid in selection for parole. But it must be conducted with an understanding of what can and cannot be expected under the conditions that prevail. Some boards allow themselves a fairly relaxed interviewing setting; others do not. Interviewing is a process which requires great skill, subtlety, and understanding. Given exceptionally experienced and knowledgeable interviewers, some of the negative physical features of the board hearing can be obviated or mitigated. But optimum results will not be achieved, certainly, until parole boards are able to schedule themselves so that they do not have to hear an impossible number of cases in one sitting.

It is an awesome experience to sit as judge of a person's fate. Effective selection for probation and parole requires wisdom, and also courage—courage to take a chance on defendant or inmate when the facts seem to warrant, and courage to say "No" when, in the interests of society, it would be unsafe to release that person to the community. Intelligence, common sense, understanding, objectivity, and courage—these are the attributes of the competent judge and parole board member.

9

RESEARCH ON SELECTION

What criteria for selection are derived from research? Prediction table studies as well as other investigations contribute the following:

1. The younger the offender, the less his chance of successful completion of probation or parole, all else being equal. (A "successful" history is usually defined in the research as nonrecidivism to delinquency or crime or to general violation of the rules and regulations of probation and parole.)

Everybody is young before he is old. Do the studies suggest that youth is an affliction, that its possessor should be ineligible for probation or parole? Of course not. Allied with constructive factors, youthfulness offers hope of readjustment before habits become too firmly rooted. Allied with destructive elements, however, it may spell recidivism, and is likely to do so more frequently than in instances where an older person is concerned, all other factors being equal.

The Gluecks noted this.[1] They found a high failure rate among their youthful offenders. It persisted until maturity set in. Then recidivism reached a plateau and remained there. Maturation in itself, they concluded, aids in the process of personal stabilization. To say that youthfulness is conducive to recidivism is equivalent to asserting that a young person must mature in order to achieve his optimum judgment and stability.

[1] Sheldon Glueck and Eleanor T. Glueck, *500 Criminal Careers* (New York: Alfred A. Knopf, 1930).

2. More significant than age alone is the age at onset of delinquency or criminality. Research indicates that the person who begins his illegal behavior early in life is less likely to succeed on probation or parole than one who commits his first offense at about age thirty or above.

3. Marital status is related to outcome. The married individual, living with his spouse, is a better statistical risk than one who is single, separated, divorced, or widowed.

4. Recidivism breeds recidivism. The offender with a long record of arrests and convictions is a less favorable risk than the first offender, a fact judges and parole boards suspected before research confirmed their educated guess. Prediction tables show that first and occasional offenders are better risks than inveterates. Authorities, then, are justified if they favor the first offender over the habitual in selection for probation or parole. It must never be forgotten, however, regarding this or any other factor, that individual exceptions to research conclusions will always exist.

5. What about conduct in the institution? Is it significant? Does it foreshadow outcome on parole? The evidence is not altogether conclusive, but most of it is to the effect that, considered per se, the inmate who behaves inside is more likely to do so on the outside than is the prisoner who chalks up a bad institutional record.

6. As indicated in the previous chapter, employment habits prior to conviction are highly predictive. The individual with good working habits who has been fairly regularly employed, and who has a job upon coming under supervision, is a better risk than one whose history shows chronic unemployment or only sporadic employment, and who has no job at the time he begins his probation or parole period.

7. There are still those who believe that so-called "race" [2] and nativity are indicative of ultimate adjustment. The foreign

---

[2] "So-called" because there is no pure race. We are all mixtures.

born are supposedly poorer risks than the native born. Negroes allegedly recidivate more frequently than whites.

Probably no statistics are as valueless as those dealing with this subject. "Race" and nationality are themselves categoric risks. To be a Negro or foreign born renders one more susceptible to arrest, conviction, and incarceration. Prejudice, if it exists, is not the only factor involved. Variables that cannot be ruled out or properly weighted are enforcement policies, attitudes of police and judges, and social conditions generally. In any event, there is nothing to support the thesis that the foreign born, or Negroes, are less deserving of probation and parole than native-born whites.

The figures do show that Negroes are *recorded* as committing a disproportionate number of crimes per capita, but the statistics mean nothing unless we know what it is impossible to know—the degree of categoric risk involved in being a Negro. Orientals seem remarkably law-abiding. Evidence is that the foreign born are less given to crime than the native born, more particularly, the native-born offspring of foreign parentage.

8. There is much folklore about patterns of offense and recidivism. Persons who use guns are supposedly more inveterate than those who do not. Sex offenders are believed to be incorrigible and terribly dangerous.

Here is what we learn from research:

Other things being equal, individuals who commit offenses against property are less successful on probation and parole than those who perpetrate offenses against the person. The forger is a poor risk, tending to bear out the folk saying, "Once a forger, always a forger." The great majority of sex offenders do not repeat their crimes or delinquencies. However, the minority, that is, compulsive sex deviates, are highly recidivistic.

9. What do we know about education as a predictive factor?

The evidence is contradictory. The Gluecks discovered no demonstrable difference between the poorly and the better educated person in so far as parole outcome was concerned. But those in their study group who did well on probation had more schooling than those who did not.[3] How interpret that?

Monachesi thought he had indication that the best probation risks were those with no education, those who had completed no more than the first to the fourth grade—and those who had finished college.[4]

10. What about intelligence? Given a feeble-minded man and one with an I.Q. of 150, is it safe to assume that the latter has a better chance of adjustment than the former? By no means. There is some conflicting evidence, but most research is in agreement that intelligence, as reflected in test scores, has no predictive value. The very bright and the very dull appear about equally successful on probation and parole.

11. Is the period of incarceration a factor in parole outcome? (The probationer, of course, has not been imprisoned for the present offense.) We hear from some that the trouble with our penology is we treat people too leniently. We lock them up on Monday, swing the doors open Tuesday, so what can we expect? If prisoners got some real seasoning, they'd learn their lesson, come out and march down the straight and narrow path forever after. Given slap-on-the-wrist treatment, naturally they laugh at courts, probation, parole.

Contra this plaint is the cry that correctional institutions can do nothing but harm prisoners. They harden them, make them worse than they were when they came in. The longer the term, the tougher the product.

What can we believe?

With some exceptions, research supports the thesis that long

[3] Sheldon Glueck and Eleanor T. Glueck, *Criminal Careers in Retrospect* (New York: Commonwealth Fund, 1943).

[4] Elio D. Monachesi, *Prediction Factors in Probation* (Hanover, N.H.: Sociological Press, 1932).

terms yield recidivism. Tibbits's work is representative. He found that offenders who had served the longer terms were more likely to violate parole than those who had served less time.[5] Burgess came to a similar conclusion, finding that the longer a prisoner remains incarcerated the less likely he is to adjust on parole.[6]

12. Do country boys do as well on parole or probation as their city cousins? It seems that this factor, taken by itself, is not very helpful in prediction. It makes little difference whether the individual concerned is country- or city-bred. What does matter is whether, relatively late in his life, the offender is transplanted. Clark reports on a study of 9,444 prisoners who were paroled from the Menard and Joliet branches of the Illinois State Penitentiary. Those sent to a community roughly the same size as the one from which they had come had a lower violation rate than inmates paroled to a community of a radically different size. The assumption is that it is easier to adjust in a familiar than in an unfamiliar milieu.[7] More comprehensive investigation might throw further light on this subject. Can children be transplanted more safely than adults? May it be that, whatever the offender's age at time of transplantation, the telling factor with which this must be coupled is the total time he spent in the original environment? An individual who spent twenty of his thirty years in a rural setting perhaps would find it harder to adjust in a metropolis than one who had spent five of those thirty years there.

13. We do not know the full meaning of it, but studies suggest that the higher the socioeconomic status of a probationer's or parolee's family, the more likely he is to succeed under supervision.

[5] C. Tibbits, "Success or Failure on Parole Can Be Predicted," *Journal of Criminal Law and Criminology*, XXII, No. 1 (1931), 11–50.

[6] E. W. Burgess, "Factors Determining Success or Failure on Parole," *Journal of Criminal Law and Criminology*, XIX No. 2 (1928), 241–86.

[7] Robert E. Clark, "Size of Parole Community, as Related to Parole Outcome," *American Journal of Sociology*, LVII, No. 1 (1951), 43–47.

10

THE HELPING PROCESS

The selective process of probation and parole completed, there begins the period of supervision and treatment, although generally the term "supervision" is used to denote both activities.

What are the supervisory functions of a probation or parole agency?

There are two: protecting the community and helping individuals under care. Each function is inextricably bound up with the other. The officer wants to safeguard society against the potential recidivist. At the same time, he hopes to help the probationer or parolee become law-abiding and stable. He removes from the community those who are an immediate danger. But the most effective community protection is that which results from change within the offender, so that he no longer wants to aggress against society.

How do we help?

In the main, we do it by casework treatment. The term "treatment," as used throughout this volume, refers to the application of casework techniques by a professional worker who seeks to help someone solve his problems.

The probation and parole officer utilizes not only casework but any and all techniques within his competence. This may include social group work (to be discussed later) and community organization. Nevertheless the earliest efforts to help offenders were neither casework nor group work. A glance backward will place contemporary methods in perspective and indicate the degree to which treatment has moved in other directions.

From Old to New

The rise of humanitarianism, it was pointed out, contributed to the development of correctional services. Basically, humanitarianism is the devotion of man to the welfare of mankind. But its doctrine of equalitarianism taught that man is born free, and is master of his destiny in a democratic society. Because he has freedom of action in attaining his goals he must be held responsible for those acts. Individual freedom and responsibility walk hand in hand. Consequently, the offender was to be held accountable by his fellow men when in pursuit of his own happiness he impaired theirs.

At times this philosophy had a stern moral cast. A physician addressing the 1883 National Conference of Charities and Correction characterized prisoners as individuals "whose 'moral sense' is weak, whose consciences are perverted, without self-control, with no will to do right." While, it was suggested:

It evidently is the duty of a Christian people to surround the weak and wicked with every helpful influence . . . let us not for a moment indulge in a sentimental hope that kind treatment, cleanly surroundings and the reposing of confidence in such unworthy objects will of itself elevate and change their evil natures.[1]

But along with such notions were to be found others that emphasized more positive approaches to treatment. At conferences where correctional workers gathered in the 1880s and 1890s speakers recommended medical care, proper diet, religious instruction, "moral elevation," vocational training, and habituation to good habits of behavior. One conferee saw value in permitting female prisoners to "keep house" and decorate

[1] Eliza M. Mosher, M.D., "Discipline in Prisons," in *Proceedings of the Tenth Annual National Conference of Charities and Correction, 1883* (Madison, Wis.: Midland Publishing Co., 1884), p. 216.

their quarters attractively. She bespoke the therapeutic effects
of music:

Let me hear the songs . . . a girl naturally sings, and I can tell
you her history and her heart. . . . Teach good national songs, and
new, sweet, helpful, prayerful songs. . . . Move to the time of
music as much as possible. . . . Drill with music. . . . It cultivates
self respect.[2]

The penal reformer Frederick H. Wines declared that "the
means to be employed for the reformation of the prisoner are
three: labor, education, and religion."[3]

Early efforts at helping conceived of the process as a direct,
administrative matter. The workers did the work. They did
things to and for offenders. Not until later did there emerge
the conception that the individual offender had to contribute
something to the treatment situation, too. Wines was one of
the first to say it: "The cooperation of the prisoner himself in the
effort to accomplish his moral renovation is indispensable to
success."[4] A prisoner said it even better:

The central truth of reformation is this: *The desire to reform must
come from within, and the degree of the accomplishment of this
desire is directly proportionate to the degree of liberty you give the
criminal to live aright and to the adequacy of his environment to
sustain this desire.*[5]

This statement points up the fact that behavior both shapes
and is shaped by the human personality; that a desire to change
must come from within; and that the environment is potent in
stimulating and sustaining that desire. That is the position of
the modern caseworker.

And so it was that, in time, with enriched knowledge from

[2] E. A. Hall, "Reformation of Criminal Girls," *ibid.*, p. 198.
[3] Frederick H. Wines, "Reformation as an End in Prison Discipline," in
Proceedings of the National Conference of Charities and Correction, 1888
(Boston: Geo. H. Ellis, 1888), p. 193.
[4] *Ibid.*, p. 194.
[5] Anonymous, *An Open Letter to Society from Convict 1776*, p. 133.

biology, psychology, sociology, and other fields, the proceedings of correctional conferences took on new slants, incor-
porating this conception. By the 1930s, we were listening to
papers on:

Can We Change Personality?
Helping the Client to Find Himself
Understanding the Delinquent
Early Treatment of Problem Children
Mental Hygiene Frontiers in Probation and Parole Services
Underlying Social Causes of Crime
Motivating the Delinquent to Accept Treatment

We had, in short, moved to a position where we recognized
the interrelatedness of personality and environment. But while
we spoke of casework techniques and psychiatric interpreta-
tions of behavior, a great deal of the professional literature of
the 1930s was still nonscientific in outlook. There was much in-
spirational material based on hunch rather than evidence. A
certain intransigence developed between those who wanted
proof and those who insisted their asserted facts were self-
evident. But gradually, throughout the decade, ideas contributed by trained workers began trickling into the correctional
field. Numerically, the persons making these contributions were
unimportant, but their influence was deeply felt. Their numbers
increased and continue to increase.

One of the forces which encouraged this infiltration of ideas
was the unlamented depression which broke upon the world
in 1929. The imperative demand for immediate development of
social services that would maintain the breath of life called for
courageous improvisation. More than that, it focused attention
on public welfare services, since private agencies could not
carry the load. And with the birth and growth of public assistance and other agencies under the Social Security Law,
professional casework began entering not those areas alone, but
all of the public social services, including corrections. The new

arrivals quickly began experimenting with adaptations of generic practices to the new setting.

Examination of the files of *Federal Probation* shows this emerging emphasis, particularly since 1950. Among the subjects covered are:

The Authority Aspect of the Worker-Client Relationship: Asset or Liability?
Setting the Sights for Delinquency Research
Therapeutic Use of Authority
An Experiment in Group Counseling with Male Alcoholic Inmates
Vandalism as an Outlet for Aggression
Social Work Principles in Probation
A Life Adjustment Class in a Reformatory Setting
A Study of Postprobation Recidivism among Five Hundred Federal Offenders
The Prison as a Therapeutic Community
The Self-Image and Delinquency: Some Implications for Religion
Crime Causation: Research and Its Application
Short-Term Treatment of Women: an Experiment

It has taken a century, but at least a great many workers in probation and parole agree that individualization of the offender, implicit in casework treatment, is a *sine qua non*. Most would probably accept today what Thomas Mott Osborne, the controversial warden of Sing Sing, wrote back in 1916:

Here . . . is the crux of the problem. Ever since the good quakers [*sic*] of Pennsylvania abolished capital punishment in 1794 we have been theorizing about criminals; and in all the dreary theorizing, and in all the hideous cruelties perpetrated in punishing men who would not adapt themselves to the various theories, and in all the weary volumes in which these futile theories are duly tabulated and explained, the one great fundamental truth has never seemed to make itself felt: that every man who is in need of reform requires a different treatment from all other men. As there are no two men alike, there is no theory that will fit them all, except the theory that they are all different.[6]

[6] Thomas Mott Osborne, *Society and Prisons* (New Haven: Yale University Press, 1916), p. 221.

Modern Orientations to Casework Treatment

How do we treat? It is impossible to impart skills in a book. They are developed in supervised field training. The most that can be done here is to present some concepts and principles useful to the correctional worker.

First, what is social casework?

It is a process in which the worker, by means of a professional relationship, works toward the ultimate aim of effecting in the person under care an adjustment to his social situation and himself which will permit him to live more comfortably with himself and among others.

It is aptly stated: "The nucleus of the casework event is this: A *person* with a *problem* comes to a *place* where a *professional representative* helps him by a given *process*." [7]

What is the purpose of casework? As our definition indicates, the objective is to help individuals solve problems, so that they may function more effectively and contentedly.

What, in broad terms, is the method of casework? Bowers defines it this way:

Social casework is an art in which the knowledge of the science of human relations and skill in relationship are used to mobilize capacities in the individual and resources in the community appropriate for better adjustment between the client and all or any part of his total environment.[8]

This knowledge is derivative in part. Casework borrows from biology, anthropology, sociology, psychology, psychiatry, and other disciplines. Out of its own practice, casework develops theory which is more than the sum of its borrowings.

The casework method involves a one-to-one relationship. There is a worker and a client, in mutual interaction. The word

[7] Perlman, *Social Casework, a Problem-solving Process*, p. 4.
[8] Swithun Bowers, "The Nature and Definition of Social Casework," in Cora Kasius, ed., *Principles and Techniques in Social Casework* (New York: Family Service Association of America, 1950), p. 127.

"client" suggests a voluntary applicant. The man seeking financial aid comes voluntarily to a public assistance agency. The
woman who wants help in resolving domestic problems voluntarily applies at a family service organization. Is the probationer or parolee a client in that sense? Not precisely. However,
the choice the offender makes to accept probation—or parole—
is a choice of sorts. Once under care, he may voluntarily seek
help toward the alleviation of certain problems, or choose not to
do so. He may not be entirely happy about rules and regulations,
yet eagerly solicit assistance in getting work or receiving medical care or in deciding whether to marry. In this area of the
casework relationship the offender is a client precisely like the
applicant of the relief or family service agency.

The casework process is one of problem-solving. Many probationers and parolees want help in solving problems. The
method used by the officer is facilitated by techniques. Techniques are the learned ways by which "a principle of methodology is translated into action." [9]

Fundamentally, there are two approaches to casework treatment in probation and parole. The environment may be manip-
ulated in the interest of the individual; and the individual may
be treated so that he may more effectively cope with his
environment. Actually, of course, no dichotomy exists. The two
approaches are not mutually exclusive. Environment fashions
personality, and personality changes environment. However,
the probation or parole officer may, at a given time, be addressing himself primarily to environmental or personal aspects
of a case.

From another point of departure, casework may be said to
consist of two problem-solving processes: the rendering of
concrete services and helping people solve inter- and intra-
personal problems. Roughly, we are distinguishing here be-

[9] Perlman, *op. cit.,* p. 158.

tween the tangible and the intangible, the sociological and the psychological approach.

There have been three discernible influences in modern casework thinking in the United States. Mary Richmond's *Social Diagnosis*, published in 1917, had a tremendous impact. The functional and diagnostic schools of thought made their highly important contributions beginning in the 1930s.

Mary Richmond asserted that the basic aim of social work was the development of personality. She defined casework as "those processes which develop personality through adjustments consciously effected, individual by individual, between men and their social environment." [10] To further this kind of practice, Richmond urged careful investigation, followed by a diagnosis of the situation so that treatment might follow. Social diagnosis was the central point of the casework situation— derived from investigation and pointed at treatment:

Social diagnosis is the attempt to arrive at as exact a definition as possible of the social situation and personality of a given client. The gathering of evidence, or investigation, begins the process, the critical examination and comparison of evidence follows, and last come its interpretation and the definition of the social difficulty.[11]

This genre of casework will probably always be indispensable in probation and parole. Correctional workers investigate to learn which offenders may properly be offered the agency's services. They check into the activities of those under supervision. They pursue social history, inasmuch as background information is essential both in selection and treatment.

Richmond said more than merely "let us investigate and diagnose." She placed emphasis upon environmental factors that shape personality. She would manipulate the environment

[10] Mary E. Richmond, *What Is Social Case Work?* (New York: Russell Sage Foundation, 1922), p. 98.

[11] Mary E. Richmond, *Social Diagnosis* (New York: Russell Sage Foundation, 1917), p. 62.

so that the client might live more comfortably and effectively
—get him relief, a job, sanitary housing, etc.

This is of the utmost importance in correctional work. Many
probationers and parolees committed their offenses when they
were no longer able to cope with environmental pressures.
Wisely proffered aid which makes the environment livable may
estop recidivism in some cases. Every man has his breaking
point. No amount of inner, psychological fortification will suffice if the environment exerts enough pressure.

Mary Richmond wrote *Social Diagnosis* before the full impact of the mental hygiene movement was felt. Her caseworker
was a doer. She went into the field, visited homes, talked with
teachers, prospective employers, clinicians. Then Freud and
psychoanalysis hit the United States with explosive force. Human personality became the focus of treatment much more
than was the case up to that time. Environmental influences
assumed a lesser importance. There emerged a reaction against
the social worker's doing to and for people. The emphasis was
on work with clients, an interactive situation in which the
client was free to make final decisions. *He* must accept responsibility for his part of the treatment process.

In psychiatry, much of what was accomplished took place
because the psychiatrist was a listener. "He did not do anything in particular to his patient. Instead he followed the lead
taken by his patient and tried to see what he could do to help
the patient help himself." Caseworkers were impressed with
this method. "The psychoanalysts all listened while their patients talked, and in talking there was therapy." [12] Caseworkers
tried to do likewise. More than before, they wanted to discover
how the client saw a situation. This was more important, at
times, than knowing what the situation was like to an objective
observer. If a woman declared her husband was unfaithful, the

[12] Herbert H. Aptekar, *The Dynamics of Casework and Counseling* (New
York: Houghton Mifflin, 1955), p. 21.

question was not, "Is this true?" so much as, "True or not, how
does the client feel about it?" Caseworkers did most of their
work in the office. They became listeners rather than doers.
They were more than sounding boards, however. They chan-
neled discussion and introspection by a judicious word or ges-
ture, or by directing a question at the client calculated to focus
attention upon a particular subject or consideration.

This understanding of the therapeutic uses of educated
listening has been of service to probation and parole officers.
They continue to do field work; they perform manipulative
services; but they have learned the value of hearing offenders,
allowing them to reveal their problems, their feelings, and
themselves in the casework relationship.

In time, psychologically oriented caseworkers split down the
middle. There were Freudians, of the diagnostic school, and
Rankians, of the functional viewpoint. Their differences are
alleged to be basic. Perhaps they are, but if so, it should be
possible to establish that one orientation yields more effective
results than the other. Despite three decades of philosophical
dispute, neither functional nor diagnostic workers have presented any research evidence to back up their claims.

For our purposes there would be little point in examining the
schools in great detail, or entering the debate on the relative
merits of the two. While no research evidence exists, observation of practice suggests that probably there are useful principles to be derived from both functionalists and diagnostic
workers. In the correctional field, where most workers do not
have the highly specialized training required for either functional or diagnostic casework, an eclectic orientation is indicated. The concepts of both schools of thought can orient the
thinking of the correctional worker even when he wisely es-
chews techniques in which he is not specifically trained. Freudian insights into the ego, superego, id, the unconscious, ambivalence, are useful in all agency settings. Rankian concepts

of the will, the importance of focusing on agency function, can also be put to use. And Richmond's thinking, with its attention to manipulation of environment, certainly has a place in the eclectic approach.

Aptekar has something like this in mind for all of social casework when he speaks for what he calls a "dynamic" approach. Its central point of emphasis must be:

> . . . neither the client, nor the agency, but instead the moving, changing, and developing interaction of one with the other. What forces does the client activate in the worker? What does he cause him to think? How does he make him feel? What action results? How does the worker appear to the client? What thoughts, feelings, and attitudes are activated within him? What mutual judging or diagnosing goes on? . . . In short, what interaction is originated in the client's and the worker's coming together? In what manner does it develop? [13]

In a dynamic approach, Aptekar suggests, the emphasis is on both client and worker, not on one or the other. The worker— and this is particularly translatable into probation and parole practice—"must be aware of divided responsibilities—those of the client as well as his own." [14] The officer has responsibilities to the agency and to the probationer or parolee. He and his charge must constantly bear this in mind.

[13] *Ibid.*, p. 78.   [14] *Ibid.*, p. 79.

11

ECLECTIC ORIENTATION IN
PROBATION AND PAROLE

Let us now consider some concepts and principles, from all schools of thought, that are of particular value in the correctional field.

1. *One human being can help another.* Were this not so, there would be no purpose whatever in the casework relationship. It has been demonstrated that a professional worker can influence the thinking, feeling, and behavior of individuals who seek help in problem-solving.

2. *Persons can be helped only if they want help.* This is not invariably the case, but the statement is sound enough as a generalization. A person can be helped if he recognizes he has a problem; sincerely wants to do something about it; feels he cannot do it alone; asks for help; is intellectually and emotionally capable of benefiting from such help; and actively cooperates in the treatment process.

Parole Officer Harrigan had under his supervision a highly intelligent man, Dr. Francis, who had been convicted of illegally performing abortions. Francis was a homosexual, frankly admitting this to Harrigan. The latter spent many hours trying to get the doctor to admit that this was a condition which would seriously impair his usefulness should he be readmitted to practice. Francis denied this, once remarking, "A doctor always divorces personal feelings from professional practice. I'm no different from the heterosexual physician who examines a woman patient."

The parole officer urged that, regardless of the doctor's feelings about implications for practice, he ought to take psychiatric treatment because his personal life would be happier if he rid himself of his homosexual urges. To this, Dr. Francis retorted, "I'm happy in my present condition. I understand it, don't fight it, and I control it. I have never shown an interest in any man who was not already a homosexual."

Had the officer succeeded in getting the doctor to recognize his homosexuality as a problem, the necessary elements for treatment might have been progressively set up. Under the circumstances, however, it would have been foolhardy for a caseworker or a psychiatrist to bludgeon his way into a putative treatment relationship. The doctor felt no travail. He did not agree he had a problem. He felt comfortable as he was.

3. *The basic tool of casework is the interview.* Treatment "happens" in the interview, which is the most important tool of the worker. Good interviewing requires the proper temperament, and the skill that comes from conscious attention to, and experience in, the process. Interviewing techniques can be learned.

4. *Personality is precious.* The interviewer who would play a helping role sincerely accepts that human personality is precious, that the dignity of man must be maintained and reinforced if he is to be able to accept needed help.

No matter what a probationer or parolee has been or has done, he must be respected as a human being, else we cannot help him. Degrading his personality never furthers casework goals. The officer's demeanor in speaking with persons under supervision reveals whether he does or does not accept this. One can be firm without being rude. To treat an ex-offender as less than human is to demonstrate that the worker has failed to understand his own function or cannot adequately perform it.

5. *The client must be accepted where he stands.* Within the limits of agency function, the officer needs to be an accepting

individual. He will not countenance or condone certain behavior, and yet he is accepting.

Peters, a tough-spoken, unlettered man of 50, had some thirty
arrests on his record, two of them leading to conviction for robbery.
Paroled, he made his arrival report to Officer Cannon, who explained
the rules and regulations. Peters indicated he understood them, but
remarked: "I'll do what you tell me, because I got to, I want to
make my parole." He was saying that he did not want to comply, but
would do so, perforce.

When the officer asked if Peters did not believe the conditions
laid down would help him, he replied in a disgusted negative.
"Look!" he went on. "Everybody's got his own self to look out for.
You know that. If you can get away with something, you do. If I
can, I do. Everybody's out for hisself."

The officer might have expressed disapproval of such cyni-
cism, but what good would it do? The mere expression would
not change the parolee's attitude. He was not ready for it. As a
caseworker, Cannon would be better advised to remain non-
committal for the time. He would accept the client where he
stood, because he could not move him forward and would build
up resistance if he tried. He might hope to help Peters gain a
different view in future, but meantime Cannon would look
upon him as an individual whom he wanted to understand, not
to change against his will. He would hold to this position so
long as Peters did not give indication he was an unsafe risk.

6. *A caseworker is nonjudgmental.* Cannon was nonjudgmental. Nonjudgmentalism is a cornerstone of casework.

"What!" the reader cries. "Do you mean to say a probation
or parole officer must never take a position that something is
good or bad?"

No, we do not mean that. Even the family service worker in
a private agency must do that at times. Suppose a client told
him he was going to murder his wife. Assume the caseworker
had reason to believe this was no rodomontade; the client

meant what he said. The agency representative might express horror, might attempt to dissuade the client. But failing that, he would take necessary steps to prevent homicide—it is to be hoped.

What, then, do we mean when we say the worker is not judgmental? We mean he does not judge the client's *feelings*, so far as the professional relationship is concerned. He assesses them, but does not moralize, order, or forbid, in so far as the *feelings* are concerned. That is, he knows he cannot rule emotions by executive fiat. He accepts them as genuine, for what they are, and makes that a beginning point for treatment. He will not legislate feelings, only acts, and then only in given circumstances.

Some acts of parolees and probationers must be regulated. The individual will not be allowed to kill or steal or beat his wife. But, if no imminent danger is foreseen, the officer will adopt no inflexible, moralistic stand, if he is wise, about the ex-offender's feelings regarding killing or stealing or beating his wife. Not that the worker has no moral positions. He certainly has, should have, and must have, in his role. But to moralize about attitudes too strenuously would defeat the aims of treatment, a treatment which will benefit society as much as the man or woman under supervision. The officer will probably control the behavioral situation where necessary while working with the individual in hopes *he* will later change his views about killing, stealing, or mayhem. It is one thing to tell a man he must not beat his wife. It is another to insist he must not want to beat her.

Some further qualification is necessary. A juvenile often lacks the judgment to know what is best for him. Like a parent, the officer will sometimes need to be quite directive. To cite an example:

Joe, age 15, had been in juvenile court many times, as a runaway and for stealing. Now he was on probation. His father was an alcoholic, his mother preoccupied with outside work, maintaining the household, and caring for five children younger than Joe. In a period of family tension, the boy irascibly reported to the officer that his father had stolen a dollar Joe had earned from his paper route. Things were going from bad to worse. Joe was going to run off again.

The officer did not argue that the home situation was ideal. But he pointed out that growing up entailed learning to adjust to the less-than-ideal.

Joe demanded, "What'll you do if I take off?"

Promptly, the officer responded, "I'll locate you and lock you up."

Discussing the case with the writer, the officer remarked, "With an adult, I would have taken more of a chance that I could talk him into seeing the danger in his frame of mind. With this particular kid, I couldn't take that chance. I had to lay down the law."

7. *Authority is a tool in casework.* Happily, the word "authority" no longer sends a shudder through the frame of the correctional worker. Earlier, he would have been impelled to go on the defensive, to insist he *had* to use authority. Yet he would have considered the entire subject a bugaboo, because he did not quite understand his own rationale in defending the use of authority. Social workers outside the correctional field made him uneasy. They insisted that casework and authority were inimical.

Today, it is the trained caseworkers who are insisting that authority, properly conceived, far from impeding the casework process, actually is an essential element in it.

When social workers, in and out of corrections, use the word "authority" today they mean something analogous to "reality," the reality situation which is presented to every one of us. We are all aware that we must face reality. All of us must work in order to eat (unless we are coupon clippers). If we do not support our dependents the law will step in and make us do so. We wear clothing, even in torrid weather, because the mores are more powerful than we. We stop at a red light because we recognize a stern reality—it is that or a ticket. All about us, in every area of endeavor, in most of what we do at work or play, we are bound by the discipline of life, and even when we sleep we do so under approved conditions. We do not lie naked in a ditch. We do things, even when we prefer not to, because it is more comfortable to conform than to suffer penalty. Most of us bow to the mores and laws of our culture. We learn to do so gladly, for the most part. We even become patriotically zealous in proclaiming this *is* the way to live. Would there not be an element of mendacity in allowing probationers and parolees to believe they are less subject to the authority of life than we? Is it not more wholesome that they understand they have a particular reality which they must face *as* probationers and parolees?

Authority in probation and parole must mean certain things to be intelligently employed:

It must not run counter to the reality situation. The officer has both a right and an obligation to insist, "You must obey the law." It is not his function to demand, "You must get a college degree."

Authority should be exercised dispassionately. It is not the officer's authority which he invokes, but society's. He is merely its representative, pointing out the reality of the situation. *He* is not saying, "Thou shalt not steal." He is asserting, "The law says you must not steal. If you do, it becomes my duty to turn you over to the police, this also according to law." The peace officer needs to be authoritative in revealing reality rather than authoritarian. What the community demands of him is that he dispassionately and sensibly enforce the *law*, not *himself*.

Which brings us to a related point. The correctional worker must be able to accept his own authority. He must not abuse it, but neither must he fear it. He must sincerely believe it is essential in casework. If he cannot accept that premise, he will not use authority effectively.

Ultimately, it must be the individual under care who chooses to accept his reality situation. Acceptance cannot be forced upon him. He alone will determine whether he is going to conform. Society will treat him one way if he does, another if he does not, and that is the reality of *that* situation.

8. *Each social agency has its particular functions and limits.* Probation and parole units are no exception. Treatment is facilitated when the person under supervision keeps this constantly in mind. It is the business of the officer to make it clear that he has certain functions and intends to exercise them; that the probationer or parolee has his obligations and must fulfill them. Both are aided if they clearly understand what are the functions of the service. Each gains a measure of security and clarity through realization of the limits that these functions necessarily impose.

The individual under supervision wants to know what the peace officer is there to do. He needs to understand what services he may get if he wishes, and what he cannot expect to receive. He must be encouraged to accept that the officer is there to aid him, along certain lines, if he wants help, but that certain limits are imposed upon both in this regard. Service to the individual will have to terminate if he gives evidence of recidivism. Whatever else the officer is there to do, he operates within that limitation—he is charged as a peace officer with protecting the community. Giving the former offender an understanding of the agency's functions and limits thus helps him crystallize his thinking as to what he must do. It makes clear to him that beyond the "musts" he may accept or reject the agency's proffered services. If he conducts himself properly he may seek assistance or not with other problems. That is up to him.

The officer serves an individual if he is able to make a certain logic clear. The agency had less to do with the offender's coming to it than that person did himself. He so acted as to bring upon himself a penalty—conviction of a crime or ad-

judication into the status of juvenile delinquent. A privilege has
been extended to him—conditional liberty. He needs to accept
the basic reality of this situation. He must remain law-abiding.
The very acceptance is growth of a sort. He then understands
he must refrain from certain activities lest they lead him into
recidivism. He may not associate with undesirable characters,
must live within his means, conduct himself with reasonable
discretion and sobriety. He must be willing to work, to support
his dependents, report to the officer when required, be frank
and not mendacious in his dealings with the latter.

The rest is voluntary. He may, after that, decide for himself
that he wants help from the officer in attacking some problem.
He will get it. He may choose to wrestle with the problem himself or go elsewhere for professional aid. That is his option.

Can an individual get casework services under such a definition of function? Yes. Every social agency has its rules of
eligibility which the client must accept if he wishes aid. That
is the reality he must face. A public assistance agency may require he furnish proof that he is without resources, or that he
will accept employment if it is found. A family service organization may specify that the client who needs guidance in
resolving an emotional problem must come at stipulated hours,
perhaps pay a fee, cooperate in the therapeutic relationship.
Probation and parole require that the recipient of service refrain from antisocial acts which may lead to recidivism. Accepting that, the probationer or parolee is eligible for other
treatment voluntarily entered into.

9. *The worker uses a self-conscious technique.* Mary is upset because she and her husband quarrel constantly. She asks a
friend what she ought to do. Should she get a divorce? Stick
it out? The friend advises her to the best of her ability. It may
turn out to be excellent counsel. It may prove, in the long run,
unwise advice, harming both parties to the dispute. Either way,
it is the advice of a lay person, based on common sense for the
most part.

Suppose Mary brought her troubles to a professional case-worker. The results might be better, or worse, than if she had gone to her friend. But they would have been achieved by a self-conscious technique. Mary's friend said what she thought, spur of the moment, whether it was wise or unwise to say so at all or to say so at that particular time. She was not conscious of a process in action between herself and Mary. The case-worker, on the other hand, has learned when to say something and when not, when to offer direct advice and when to guide the individual into his or her own insights. Whatever she does, the worker is always consciously aware why she is doing it, and why at that particular moment. She is using the self-conscious technique which, because it is based upon professional knowl-edge, is expected to yield optimum benefits.

Mrs. Carson, probation officer, visited her probationer, Alice, who was in the hospital recovering from a series of operations for rheu-matoid arthritis. Mrs. Carson knew that Alice would never regain full use of her limbs. She would always be handicapped in em-ployment. The officer also was aware that these dismal realities had not been revealed to the girl by the medical social worker, because it was felt the patient was not ready for them.

As soon as Alice saw Mrs. Carson, she cried, with irritation, "I want to go home! They're keeping me here for nothing! I'm well! My husband is begging me to come home. He's anxious to take care of me at home!"

Mrs. Carson knew that Alice's husband was not eager to have her home. He was, in fact, rather dreaming about taking up his abode with another woman and deserting his incapacitated wife entirely. Mrs. Carson, further, had a fair idea that Alice understood this, in the back of her head, but would not let her conscious self acknowl-edge it.

The officer did not say, "Alice, you will never completely recover." Nor did she tell the girl, "Your husband *isn't* anxious to have you home." Yet both of these grim realities must eventually be presented to the patient. Mrs. Carson was utilizing the self-conscious tech-nique in *not* saying certain things at this moment.

In the next several weeks, both Mrs. Carson and the medical social worker used the self-conscious technique in saying *when* it was best to help *what* realization reach the girl's consciousness. That same technique guided the workers in the manner of explanation, the supportive treatment when the facts became clear to the patient.

Eventually, Alice accepted her incapacity. She learned that her husband had actually deserted her, but found this out when she was emotionally better prepared for such brutal intelligence. She accepted the inevitable, and cooperated in arranging residence in a private home where she would be cared for to the extent required. To have proposed this earlier would have done no more than upset the girl.

The caseworker speaks, not as an authoritarian, but as a professional person with the self-conscious recognition that she has knowledge and skill beyond that of the individual in need of help. Moreover, she has been trained in the timing and method of rendering such service.

In probation and parole, dealing with juveniles and adults, the trained officer should be able to help his charges foresee the consequences of acts, to understand what is best for them under given conditions, and to make final decisions themselves after such insights have been afforded them through the self-conscious techniques of the worker.

10. *Early childhood experiences influence later behavior and attitudes.* The worker therefore inquires into background, seeking clues to what makes the man today. Much of what John Doe does and feels today is related to what happened long ago. This fact has implications for treatment. John was conditioned by a great many experiences. Somewhere along the way he learned to be willing to steal or assault or kill. The sadism which Mr. Doe manifests today may in part stem from early hostility toward a parent—or it may not. Masochism may be a symptom of the need for self-punishment arising out of guilt feelings surrounding early behavior or thoughts—but only a mountebank would hold this is always the case. No pat theory of behavior will explain all sadism or masochism or anything else.

11. *Man's behavior is influenced by unconscious as well as conscious motivation.* One of the most meaningful of Freud's many contributions is his elucidation of the role of the unconscious. We act, in part, on the basis of early influences and events which became buried in the unconscious. We are not always aware why we act as we do. Yet we behave that way because the unconscious drives us to it. Understanding what lies buried there helps us understand ourselves better.

The caseworker is not professionally equipped to work with the unconscious. This is the function of a psychiatrist, who helps a troubled person bring repressed material into the conscious realm. But the social worker gains understanding of probationers and parolees when he learns the role of the unconscious, that some behavior is symptomatic of what lies within the individual.

12. *The present and conscious situation is important in treatment too.* Freudians emphasize the diagnostic approach, delving into the past to understand the present so that they may contribute to making the future a happier one. Rankians, and practitioners of the functional school of thought in casework, do not deny the power of the unconscious when they assert that immediate facts, situations, and attitudes are also important to the individual in determining what he will do to solve his problems. Mere investigation of the past may have little value for treatment. According to the Rankian view:

. . . knowledge of the past can be helpful through understanding of the role which the past continues to play in the present. But the real past can never be duplicated. The present can be experienced, however, and through present experience in differentiating one's self from another, it is possible to understand the pattern of one's own will. Once the will is understood. . . . [one] can then be free to live it out affirmatively, or creatively.[1]

13. *Ambivalence is present in much of the person's behavior.* Every human being is ambivalent about many things. He hates

[1] Aptekar, *The Dynamics of Casework and Counseling*, p. 33.

and loves the same person at a given moment. He wants and does not want something. The ex-offender may like and dislike his officer. He may want to come to him for advice, yet fear to do so. He may hope to get along without committing crime, yet feel compelled to perpetrate at least one more.

What are the implications for treatment? The officer can help his charge understand that ambivalence is normal. This may make it easier for him to reveal and examine his ambivalence, to decide which feeling should be allowed to take on greater weight.

14. *The caseworker must know himself.* A caseworker is as human as the person with whom he deals. He likes and dislikes, in all degrees of intensity. It is not to be expected that, in dealing with probationers and parolees, the officer will always be neutral in his feelings. But the existence of strong feelings concerning some person or situation must not affect his practice. He must understand his own biases and compensate accordingly. The worker who is deeply religious must not let this affect his working relations with an atheist under his supervision. The officer constantly chafing under the goads of a termagant wife (it does happen!) cannot afford to let his feelings about termagants spill over into his professional relations with a termagant.

The fact that a professional person is aware he has some biases should preclude their being misused. But too many strong biases and problems associated with them may render a worker unable to perform satisfactorily. It is a truism of casework that the person in a helping role must have solved his personal problems reasonably well before he can help others solve theirs.

15. *Casework involves a relationship.* In fact, casework *is* a relationship. Virginia Robinson wrote that:

The case work relationship is a reciprocal relationship in which the case worker must accept herself and the other equally, in which all of her attitudes towards the client would be such that she would be content to be at the other end of such a relationship herself.[2]

This may seem a tall order for a correctional worker, who has not himself breached the law. Actually, it is not. Robinson merely means that the worker will treat the person under care with that respect which he would like shown him were the roles reversed.

What is this casework relationship which is the heart of the helping process? It is more than the business of two people being together in time and place. It is more than pleasant intercommunication.

The casework relationship begins when two people, with some common interest, long- or short-term, interact with feeling. The probationer and his officer have a common interest. Both want to see the former "make probation."

Relationship leaps from one person to the other at the moment when emotion moves between them. They may both express or invest different or even opposing emotions; or—and this is the situation in casework—one may express or invest emotion, and the other will receive it and be responsive to it. It any case, a charge or current of feeling must be experienced between two persons. Whether this interaction creates a sense of union or antagonism, the two persons are for the time "connected" or "related" to each other.[3]

The current of feeling does not run just in one direction. Both people are concerned in it, both feel it, both contribute to it. Treatment occurs in this sort of give-and-take relationship.

In probation and parole, the individual under supervision must be able to believe the officer wants to understand and help. He must feel the worker will not deliberately demean him. He must be secure in the knowledge, gained from experience in the relationship, that the officer will not go too far too fast, expect progress before the individual wants it.

[2] Virginia P. Robinson, *A Changing Psychology in Social Case Work* (Chapel Hill: University of North Carolina Press, 1930), pp. 170–71.

[3] Perlman, *Social Casework, a Problem-solving Process,* pp. 65–66.

16. *Not all people have problems and not all need help.*
Every one of us, of course, has what may be called "problems."
Most of them are solved without much pain or the uttering of
jeremiads. The car breaks down. We must get to the office.
We telephone a friend. The problem is solved.

But there are other problems, long-lasting, deep-seated, difficult of solution. Not everyone has these. Not even every person on probation or parole needs social work help. Let us not
take for granted that because an individual is in such status
he *ipso facto* requires treatment of some sort.

This consideration is all the more relevant when it is recognized that the great majority of probation and parole officers
carry staggering caseloads. A classification of cases in terms
of treatment needs can alleviate the situation.

Some probationers and parolees have no pressing discom-
forts or problems. They need and want nothing of the officer
in this respect. They are not serious risks in society, either.
The officer need only render routine supervision, keep himself
informed of their whereabouts and of their activities in general. He would want to guard against the outside possibility
of recidivism. This would make such persons almost "paper"
cases.

Some convicted persons have problems which they have
not solved. They are aware these exist, are intellectually and
emotionally capable of profiting from help, but do not want
it. It may be because they believe they can work out these
problems by themselves, or perhaps the decision to decline
help is due to a desire to hold on to some neurotic pleasure.
Perhaps the fear of the pain involved in struggling for a solution inhibits the individual. In such cases, the officer may hope
to help the person gain sufficient insight and strength to seek
a solution. If he succeeds, treatment may then begin. If not,
supervision, surveillance, and such manipulative aid as is
needed on occasion are about all the officer can undertake.

The object is only to see to it that the probationer or parolee does not injure others. The officer tries to insure community safety, but he will not invade the personal life of the individual any further.

Some individuals have problems calling for treatment, realize it, vaguely or positively feel they want to do something about it, but would be unable to profit from treatment because the roots of the difficulty are too firmly embedded, or the person is intellectually so far below average as to be incapable of taking part in a meaningful worker-client relationship. Here, the most that can be expected is that the officer will be vigilant, will try to forestall recidivism, will offer the former offender needed manipulative services. But casework going more in depth is usually out of the question.

Some probationers and parolees are troubled by problems, know it, want to do something about these problems, are capable of benefiting from casework treatment, and actively seek it. These are the persons for whom the fullest casework service is intended. They are the individuals who will receive the intensive attention of the officer. They offer the greatest hope of change. They are the group most closely analogous to the clients of private agencies. But regardless of the possibilities or course of the casework relationship, the officer will still recognize his responsibility for community protection. His casework treatment will move along with his community protection endeavors. The probationer or parolee may show progress, but if he manifests symptoms of recidivism, treatment will have to cease in the interest of community safety.

Finally, there are individuals who have problems affecting their own and the community's welfare. They may or may not be conscious of the existence of such problems. They may or may not want to come to grips with them. They may or may not be able to profit from treatment. But they all have one thing in common: they are very serious risks. Such cases must be treated primarily, and at times exclusively, as intensive supervision cases, with the emphasis upon supervision, not treatment. We will render society the service of constant surveillance and vigilance, quick action if revocation becomes essential. The law enforcement function will be paramount. Casework services will be available when wanted, but they will not be offered at the cost of relaxation of vigilance.

Cases, then, will tend to fall into groups: (1) those in which casework service is indicated as primary; (2) those in which the law enforcement function is the first, sometimes the sole consideration; (3) those cases requiring little more than paper classification and the most routine follow-up.

12

WAYS OF HELPING

Having briefly surveyed some principles useful to the helping process, let us now translate these into practice, to the limited degree possible through the written word.

Social work terminology can be confusing, since the same word may mean different things to different practitioners. To hurdle this semantic barrier, here is *this* writer's definition of terms used in this chapter. Not all social workers would agree. They are offered only as a universe of discourse here—not for external use.

1. *Manipulative techniques.*—These consist of manipulations of the environment in favor of the person seeking help. The end product is usually something material and tangible received by the individual under care: financial aid rendered by the agency; an employer persuaded to rehire a discharged worker.

2. *Executive techniques.*—The worker's activity in referring people to other resources in the community for help which his own agency cannot itself render. End products: referral to a legal aid society; securing public assistance for a client.

3. *Guidance techniques.*—Advice and personal guidance by the worker in connection with problems not requiring psychological techniques of an advanced order. The advice is likely to be fairly direct, the problem comparatively superficial. The end product is intangible, although it may facilitate the achievement of tangible goals. Example: the individual is advised how

to budget his income; he is helped to explore the possibilities
of trade training.

4. *Counseling techniques.*—These are based largely upon
psychological orientations. They require the utmost in skills.
The services are intangible, concerned with deep-seated problems in the emotional area. Examples: aid in adjusting to
married life; help in overcoming specific emotional conflict.

This classification is arbitrary and unorthodox; [1] but it attempts to differentiate techniques on the basis of the broad
orientation the worker uses in rendering particular types of
service. Thus, manipulative techniques are what might be
called "sociological." They address themselves to the client's
environment. Executive techniques are also sociologically
oriented in the main, the worker going into the community
to secure needed services. Guidance techniques involve some
psychological orientation. In utilizing counseling methods the
worker is not only psychologically *oriented*, but uses psychological *treatment processes*, although not delving as deeply as
would a psychiatrist.

Manipulative Techniques

Several studies of probation and parole outcome find the
same meaningful phenomenon: close to 60 percent of those
who will recidivate while under supervision do so in less than
a year after coming under care; about 40 percent of eventual
recidivists are declared delinquent before six months of supervision have elapsed. There are many reasons why this is so
in the individual case, but it is an observation of fieldworkers
that the probationer or parolee whose physical needs are met
upon returning to the free community is more likely to become
psychologically adjusted to freedom than one who is unemployed or in need of shelter or other material comforts.

[1] For another classification, see Aptekar, *The Dynamics of Casework and
Counseling,* particularly Chap. 4, "From Casework to Counseling."

Manipulative techniques are extremely important with the offender group, for they facilitate the solution of immediate environmental tensions which so often lead to recidivism. Bringing such relief may not solve a problem permanently, but eliminating the crisis may prevent what would otherwise be explosive, catastrophic answers to the situation.

The probation or parole officer does well to think of the beginning of the casework process as a time in which he must, as quickly as possible and in collaboration with the ex-offender, determine three things:

1. What are the individual's immediate problems?
2. What alternatives exist for solution of these problems?
3. Which seems to be the wisest alternative?

This is exemplified in the case of Steve, who was paroled from a reformatory when he was eighteen and no longer a juvenile by the laws of his state:

Steve's father was an alcoholic, his mother insane and in an institution. The father, with four children older than Steve, lived in a tenement hovel in one of the most decrepit sections of Manhattan. Every member of the household had a criminal record.

Steve made his arrival report and promptly told Mr. Cross, his parole officer, that although paroled to take up residence with his father, he had no such intention. Emotionally, he declared, "I never want to see them again! My folks are all bums!"

Whatever the officer's private opinion, the fact was the parole board had accepted the home offer only because no other was available. Cross pointed out, "You were paroled to this home, and that's where we expect you to go. We expect you at least to try to make out there."

Steve blazed, "O.K.! Send me back to the ref! If I live with those bums I'll wind up in the electric chair! So send me back now!"

Words tumbling over each other, he described how his father used to beat him; how he fed him liquor when the boy was five. He told Cross that his oldest brother inducted him into his first burglary, encouraged him to graduate to robbery.

"But where would you go?" the parole officer inquired. "You have no other home."

"I'll sleep on park benches. I'll sleep on subway platforms. I don't care where. I'll make out better that way."

In this initial interview, Officer Cross came up against an urgent problem. The parole board's approved plan probably would not be practical. He and the parolee must examine alternatives.

"All right," Cross said. "Maybe you've got good reasons for feeling the way you do. I'm glad you told me how you feel, instead of pretending you'd go home when you had no such intention."

Steve subsided.

"Let's see what we can figure out," the officer urged. Steve couldn't sleep on park or subway benches, could he? Wouldn't that lead to his arrest by police? Steve admitted the logic of that.

"And you don't really want to go back to Elmira, do you?" The parolee confessed he preferred freedom, if he could have it on his terms.

What else was left? Together, officer and parolee explored the possibilities. Steve might be referred to a residence club where his rent would go "on the cuff" until he got his first salary from the job to which he was paroled. With chagrin, Steve murmured he had an idea the job was "a phony," put up at the behest of his brother to effect the parolee's release.

Mr. Cross complimented Steve on his frankness again. He told him he might still go to the residence club, pay back rent after he had a job. He could be housed in a Salvation Army shelter, at no cost. Or he might be eligible for financial aid from the Department of Public Welfare. What did Steve think of these alternatives?

Encouraged to examine them, the youth asserted he would not run up a bill for rent without knowing he could pay. He would rather be returned to the reformatory than take free lodgings from the Salvation Army or money from "the relief." Accepting "charity" had great, negative, emotional meaning for the boy. He was almost hysterical as he spoke of his loathing of "going on charity," something to which he had never accustomed himself in the many years his family subsisted on public relief. His feelings represented a stronghold of self-respect, and the officer had no intention of storming that bastion.

"Well, Steve," he asked, "what can *you* suggest?"

The parolee considered, came up with the information he had

an aunt in the Bronx, a nice woman, with her own children. She and his father had had nothing to do with each other for years, and probably she wasn't interested in Steve, but . . .

The officer communicated with the aunt, who agreed to take Steve in, at least for the time. One pressing problem was out of the way. There was another. If Steve was to pay his way anywhere, he would have to have a job. The officer suggested the parolee try to locate something himself. He did and failed. He was thereupon referred to the employment bureau operated by the parole agency. A job was secured for him. He began paying rent to his aunt, later moved into a small apartment of his own.

In the initial interview, Mr. Cross was aware that Steve's need for home and job was neither the sole nor the most basic problem facing the boy. But it was the most immediate, and the officer chose to do first things first. After these pressures subsided, Steve would be able to give himself more readily to facing other problems, such as his feelings toward his family, his ambivalence about the kind of life he wanted to live —criminal or respectable. Years later, the parolee, reminiscing, told Mr. Cross he had no doubt that, had he been forced to return home *or* accept relief and free lodgings, he would immediately have absconded and reverted to crime.

Obviously, manipulative techniques were not the sum and substance of the casework situation here. Even at the very outset, the parole officer used other approaches. Rarely are manipulative techniques used to the exclusion of others.

Manipulative activities of a probation or parole officer include:

1. *Job-finding.*—Some correctional agencies have their own employment bureaus. Others rely upon officers' cultivating prospective employers who may be called upon in the interest of a person under supervision.

2. *Home-finding.*—Every correctional organization has in its caseload men, women, and children for whom adequate, psychologically satisfying homes must be found.

3. *Improvement of community life.*—Officers, with and some-

times without police assistance, help clean up "hot spots" which offer temptation to young and old. The removal of such areas of social contagion is a service not alone to probationers and parolees, but to the public as a whole.

Manipulative services, like any other in casework, require skill in their administration. The officer must sense when they should be rendered and when not. It is possible, by giving too readily, to make the recipient overdependent. To offer help at the wrong psychological moment may engender resistance or injure the person's dignity. The self-conscious approach of the skilled worker is as necessary in the manipulation of the environment as in any other technique for helping. The officer will want to ask: Is this the time to step in? What will it mean to this person? What may it do for and to him? The objective of sound manipulative work is not to take the problem away from the individual seeking assistance, but to help him mobilize his own capacities to meet his environment, so far as possible. The worker brings about change in environmental conditions only if the probationer or parolee cannot do so himself, and when receiving help will not cripple the recipient so that he will begin to use the worker as a crutch. The utilization of manipulative techniques is not simple:

Help needs to be forthcoming without too great a struggle on the individual's part, but so far as possible only at the time when it does not signify to the recipient that he has failed once more to meet one of life's realities. Even in the use of manipulative services, the individual must, so far as is feasible, feel that he played a meaningful role.[2]

Executive Techniques

No social agency can furnish all the services any client will need. Therefore, executive techniques are brought into play. To refer intelligently, the worker must know his community

[2] Dressler, *Probation and Parole*, p. 162.

and where he can go for what. Among the executive services provided by an agency representative are:

1. *Job secural.*—If the correctional agency does not have its own placement service, referral is made to public and private employment agencies.

2. *Relief.*—The officer needs to know when someone under his care is eligible for financial assistance and where he can get it.

3. *Medical-dental care.*—Probationers and parolees often must make use of clinics, hospitals, psychiatrists, dentists. It may be necessary for the officer to provide information concerning the resources available to them.

4. *Social insurances.*—The Social Security Law is complicated. If the officer understands it he can refer those persons eligible for unemployment benefits, old age insurance, and survivors' benefits. The permanently and totally disabled are entitled to certain special consideration under the law, but funds will not be drawn to the individual's benefit unless proper application is made. Many people let their rights in these matters go by default, because they do not understand the law. The officer has an obligation to guide those under supervision so that they may derive the benefits the law contemplates.

5. *Special diet.*—Children, the sick, the elderly, frequently require special diets and instruction in their use. Most cities of any size have agencies providing these services, with which the worker will be familiar.

6. *Testing services.*—Psychometric examination may be indicated for juveniles. Aptitude testing helps young and old discover their vocational talents. Educational achievement tests are excellent diagnostic devices which aid in planning school careers.

7. *Institutional placement.*—Orphanage, rest home, or other institutional care may solve some problems of the probationer or parolee.

8. *Foster home placement.*—This may be advised for a juvenile under supervision or for the child of an adult probationer or parolee.

9. *Nursery care.*—Working parents who make use of this service may need to be informed of available facilities.

10. *Legal aid.*—Marriages get mixed up. Bigamous relationships existing prior to the supervision period must be straightened out. Custody or support of children may be at issue. Divorces, annulments, and legal separations must at times be effected. Civil actions against, or on behalf of probationers and parolees require professional service from the worker.

11. *Recreation.*—Officers can stimulate interest in wholesome leisure-time activities, cultural and recreational. Settlement houses, community centers, parks, playgrounds, may be used for this purpose.

12. *Other social services.*—The wise correctional worker knows his own functions and limitations within the agency structure. In most instances, he is neither expected nor trained to furnish the kind of treatment which is carried on in child guidance clinics, psychiatric social work agencies, and family service organizations established to deal in considerable depth with emotional problems. Referral is the answer to such needs.

Executive services do not amount to a parceling out of aspects of a case, each to be treated *in vacuo.* The officer does not surrender responsibility for a case when he makes a referral. The latter is part of an over-all plan. The referred service supplements the officer's efforts, the agencies concerned working together toward common ends.

Guidance Techniques

In furnishing guidance toward the solution of problems, the worker uses as background his knowledge of the mainsprings of behavior. He is expected to know something about human motivation, what man seeks in life, how he reacts to frustration, how he goes about solving his problems. In guidance work, as we have defined it for purposes of this discussion, the officer inevitably must deal with psychological needs. His principal tools are his knowledge, his professional skill, and the casework interview.

In interviewing, he is no mere sounding board, but an active participant. The probationer or parolee has come to him for help. That help will emerge from the face-to-face relationship, in which emotion flows both ways. The person seeking guidance expresses his need, his feelings, while the worker responds with interest, understanding, judicious questions, brief comment or direct advice, appropriately timed.

The worker helps the client articulate his thoughts and feelings, then aids him in mobilizing the strength he has or can be helped to summon to meet his problems realistically. Thus, the officer contributes a great deal more than a receptive ear and responsive conversation. He has greater detachment than the person with the problem. He can present situations in perspective, where the probationer or parolee may be too emotionally involved to do so. The officer may make concrete suggestions which illuminate the issues and point to available alternatives toward the solution of the matter at hand.

Sometimes this guidance is firm, even unequivocal, as when it is necessary to say what conduct will and what will not be sanctioned, what action will lead to revocation and what to continued freedom. This is particularly necessary with young people, who profit from direct injunction when they cannot themselves readily foresee the consequences of their acts.

There is one aspect of treatment in a correctional setting which is not often encountered in voluntary social agencies. In many instances, the probationer or parolee does not want to be there, except that he has the choice of that or incarceration. He may be suspicious of, antagonistic toward, the very person who wants to help him readjust his life to the realities of social existence. It helps when both the worker and his charge frankly recognize this fact and accept it as normal. The air is cleared when the probationer or parolee finds himself free to express resentment or irritation. It is further cleared when the officer delineates the two areas in which the relationship operates. In one, certain "givens" must be accepted —the person under supervision is not to violate the law, he shall observe certain standards of behavior. The other area consists of those behaviors and tendencies to behave which do not presage violation of probation or parole. This area houses the emotional problems concerning which the individual may voluntarily seek help.

It comes clear: whether the person under supervision accepts the rules and regulations emotionally or not, they are, to the stipulated degree, immutable. They were created neither by the worker nor by the person under care. But they are there. On the other hand, a broad range of services is available to those who wish to avail themselves of them, and here the relationship is voluntary and fraught with no peril so far as maintenance of probation or parole status is concerned.

Willie, age 11, became a ward of the juvenile court when he was picked up as a runaway. Investigation disclosed he was a chronic truant, and his schoolwork was far below par.

Willie's parents proved to be unwilling or unable to supervise him. The father was a chronic deserter. The mother, formerly a nurse, was drug-addicted from time to time. In between sanitarium stays, she was an inadequate housekeeper and mother.

The juvenile court ordered Willie placed in a foster home for a trial period. Psychometric examination disclosed that the boy had a phenomenally high I.Q. He was capable of doing good work at school, if motivated.

At the beginning of the relationship between probationer and officer, the lad was noncommunicative, evasive, and untruthful. After two months, the officer remarked, "You don't like coming here, do you Willie?"

The boy flushed, but said nothing. The officer continued: "I can understand that. Most of the fellows are like that when they first come here. I know how you feel."

Willie still made no response. The probation worker said he understood the boy didn't like being told what to do. Most kids were like that.

Willie remarked he didn't mind reporting. The officer was "all right." But: "Every step I take, there's probation hanging over me. I can't do this and I mustn't do that!"

"Do you mean," the worker asked, "that you're afraid of me?" That was it, Willie agreed. The officer was the law, and that was to be feared. He didn't like being "followed by the law." Sure! He'd misbehaved. Had he kept going that way he would be in greater trouble today. But he didn't think he had much chance of straightening out when he had to watch his step every minute, lest he be considered a probation violator.

Quietly, the officer explained the obligations placed upon him by the court, that he did have the function of checking on Willie's behavior. He also recapitulated for the boy the obligations of a probationer. Certain behavior would, in truth, not be countenanced. Willie must attend school regularly. He must remain in his foster home. He must be off the streets at night. And he must be truthful with the officer even when telling the truth was painful or frightening.

"Is that so very hard?" the probation officer inquired.

"No," Willie grudgingly agreed.

If, the worker continued, Willie resented him, it was quite all right to say so. If he disagreed about something, that was understandable. No penalty would attach to it. So what really bothered Willie?

The youngster shrugged, unable to express what was on his mind. But from that time on, the officer noted, there was a change in Willie's demeanor in the office. He was more friendly, more outgoing, less evasive. He relaxed during interviews, even laughed, and evidenced a delightful sense of humor and capacity for gaiety.

Taking another step forward, the officer made clear that as long as Willie followed the rules laid down, within reason, nothing more would be demanded. Beyond that, if he had anything bothering him, if he wanted help, the officer would do his best. In one interview, it was pointed out to the boy that he had a fine mind, perhaps was bored at school because he was ahead of the class. His excellent mentality, the worker remarked, made people feel Willie could and would become a fine, useful citizen.

To this, the young fellow replied, "I want to be an astronomer!"

This led to a discussion of astronomy. Willie forgot himself as he enthusiastically talked about mathematics, the charting of stars, the solar system. "Astronomy," he declared, "isn't a useless science! People think it is, but it isn't!"

The relationship became warmer and more meaningful than before. Willie accepted the opportunity to discuss astronomy with a near-by university professor. The latter emerged, after a two-hour session, shaking his head with incredulity. "That boy," he asserted, "knows more astronomy than I do!"

Willie made regular visits to the professor thereafter. He discussed ways and means of getting to college, so he could become an astronomer.

Of his own accord, he told the officer he felt the urge to run off again. He didn't like his foster parents. They didn't understand kids. The worker thanked Willie for bringing this matter up voluntarily. Rules and regulations were involved, both agreed. But personal feelings, too, merited consideration. Would Willie face up to the fact that everybody had to take some bitter with the sweet? Would he stick it out at least until the officer had a better chance to study the home situation? Willie said he would guarantee that.

The trouble, it seemed, was that the foster parents did not have the ability to cope with the special needs of a brilliant child. They disapproved of Willie's spending hours at night, in the back yard, staring at the stars. They didn't discourage his desire to do odd jobs so he could save money, but they definitely frowned upon his plan to use that money for the purchase of a telescope. What did a kid need with an expensive gadget like that?

Attempts were made, with the cooperation of Willie, to bring about some *rapprochement*, but obviously they were going to fail. The university professor expressed a desire to take the boy. He had no children and his wife was unable to bear any. They missed having a family. They believed they had the necessary objectivity, at the same time, not to involve themselves and Willie in an affectional relationship which would make it the more difficult for the boy eventually to return to his own parents.

Arrangements were effected. Willie was told he might change

homes. His reaction was, "I'm scared. Like I was when I first met you."

"Why?" the probation worker wanted to know.

"I *like* the professor! I want him to like me. I'm afraid I won't behave so he *will* like me."

But things worked out splendidly. However, Willie now brought other problems to the probation office. He was very self-conscious about his diminutive size. He wondered whether he was a dwarf. This had been on his mind a long time, and it evidenced progress that at last he could discuss it. Further, he was worried about his eyes, which were corrected by glasses. Could a fellow become an astronomer if he had to wear glasses?

There were other problems, from time to time, now discussed without reticence—and without fears about rules and regulations. Willie didn't have to worry about rules. He was doing fine.

Gradually, he was encouraged to transfer his problem-solving relationship to his foster parents. The boy's mother died in a sanitarium, and the father promptly deserted his children, never to be heard from again. Willie remained with the professor until ready to matriculate at college. His objective had changed by then. He wanted to be a physicist—which he is today.

Processes we discussed earlier are exhibited in this case. The officer did not go in depth to the extent he might had he been trained in particular psychological practices. But he did utilize psychological concepts toward an understanding of Willie. In his own way, by means of fairly superficial guidance techniques, the probation officer clarified the role of the agency, helped Willie strengthen his ego structure and find his balance.

Probationers and parolees can be helped through the sensible, mature, understanding guidance of the worker, whether or not he is academically or otherwise equipped to use techniques derived from Freudian, Rankian, or other psychological thinking. This can occur if the officer does no more than explore a problem with the person under care, help him see the pros and cons, guide him toward insights which will bring a wise decision as to the path to follow.

But guidance does not consist simply of giving advice or

helping people come to their own decisions. The individual must be aided to walk away from the worker when the time has arrived for it. The worker must not be a crutch, but a catalytic agent. Of what utility is treatment if it leaves the person in a dependent relationship? The mature, healthy person is one who has learned not only to solve a given problem, but to solve his problems *generally*, on his own. Willie was encouraged to exchange his relationship with the probation officer for the more normal one with foster parents. And those parents were sensible enough not to tie the boy to their emotional apron strings forever. When he was strong enough to go to college, they helped him walk away and become his own man.

The guidance technique is effective only if the worker recognizes how far he can go, and what he is equipped to do. It is not psychiatry. It is not what this author means by a counseling technique.

Counseling Techniques

Little space is devoted here to counseling techniques because few correctional workers are trained in this method, which goes deeper into an exploration of emotional difficulties than any described up to this point. Where staff has the requisite training, such counseling can be effective. Otherwise, it is dangerous. Not every medical man is a surgeon, and unless he is he does not perform surgery. Not every person engaged in a helping profession is trained in therapeutic techniques derived from psychology, psychiatry, or psychoanalysis. If not, he must eschew working with techniques in which he has not interned. They cannot be learned from books or via lectures. They are gained by supervised field training, under the auspices of a graduate school of social work. Those who have such training do not need to have it discussed here. Those who have not had it, cannot get it from this printed page. This is in no sense a derogation of the worth of those correctional workers who have not had this specific orientation and supervised practice.

Most probation and parole officers can and do make a sound, solid contribution in the helping area. The author is merely suggesting that a little knowledge is a dangerous thing, and that officers do best when they use those techniques concerning which they have more than a little knowledge and skill.

Group Work Techniques

So far, we have dealt exclusively with casework services. Group techniques have latterly been introduced in institutional settings and also in parole and probation to some extent.

In casework, the professional person involves himself and client in a one-to-one relationship. In group work, the worker is related to a group of people. Two broad areas of group work exist. In one, a worker helps people gain satisfactions and self-development through group associations, in community centers, settlement houses, and the like. One characteristic that differentiates such activity from casework is that most of the participants in group activities of the sort indicated are not troubled by problems related to those activities. They do not seek out the worker for purposes of treatment. They come to have a good time, to receive intellectual stimulation, to participate in athletics.

The second kind of group work is group therapy. Here the group members do have problems. But sometimes they either are not fully aware they have them or, if they are, may not want to resolve them. The professional worker's role includes making the group members aware of their problems and desirous of working on them. And the treatment flows, not so much from worker to individual and back, in mutual interaction. Rather, the worker stimulates group members to discuss their mutual problems among themselves. He channels the discussion, helps members understand its meaning, pulls the ends together finally. He, like the caseworker, is a catalyst.

The group worker in a community center or similar organization is a social worker. Group therapy requires other skills. For such work institutions and agencies enlist psychiatrists, psychologists, and psychiatric social workers who understand group therapy techniques.

Both types of group work are to be found in probation and parole. Officers sometimes organize and lead recreational and cultural activities in communities, with the calculated aim of drawing in ex-offenders, particularly the younger ones. Group therapy is much more sparingly used in probation and parole. It is only recently being experimented with in a few places.

More common, and serving as a guide line, is group therapy in institutions. During the Second World War the therapy was used with military personnel, individual treatment being too costly and time-consuming. Among offenders in service, it was reported that personality characteristics sometimes appeared modified. "The belligerent, overassertive, antisocial rehabilitee is brought into line by his fellows and the asocial, shy, withdrawn person is drawn into conversation." [3]

From military settings, group therapy came into experimental use in civilian prisons and reformatories. Under the guidance of the therapist, prisoners engaged in the highly personal and painful business of discovering, among themselves, why they aggressed against society. In a highly permissive atmosphere, inmates helped each other gain understanding.

Criminality and delinquency are social in nature; that is, they develop out of human interaction. It may be reasoned, therefore, that such behavior can be modified if the offender's relations with social groups are modified. Group sessions in institutions are devoted to helping individuals find their way to approved relationships with others in society. Members of the group find socially approved values to replace the disapproved.

[3] Joseph Abrahams, M.D., and Lloyd W. McCorkle, "Group Psychotherapy of Military Offenders," *American Journal of Sociology*, LI, No. 5 (1946), 458.

The dynamics of a group therapy session are illustrated below. The excerpt deals with the twelfth professionally led meeting of a group of young offenders, as reported by the Director of the Highfields Project, Hopewell, New Jersey:

Pat and Charles started to talk about how the group had been silent most of the time the last few meetings. The leader said he had noticed this and wondered if they could think of any reasons why they were unable to talk. Several of the members said it was difficult to "start talking." Frank said the problem was "to get started." Carl said, "This puzzles me. What are we supposed to do in here? So far all I've heard is a lot of bitching or else everyone keeps quite." [Sic.] Frank said "You're supposed to talk about your problems." Pat said he wished the group would "get started" because "I want to make some progress and get out of this place."

The leader asked the group what they thought Pat needed to learn. Charles said, "I knew him outside and he was pretty lazy. He's not lazy in here but he couldn't keep a job out there. I think that's what he needs." Pat did not say anything, looked at the floor, moved his feet about.

The leader asked Bill what he thought about Charles's observations about Pat. Bill replied, "You know what I thought? I thought he was a squealer and they're supposed to be friends and he told about him not working outside." When the leader asked Bill why he felt so strongly about this, he replied, "I don't think anybody ought to say that. I don't want anybody to say anything like that about me. If you want to know those things, I'll tell you. I think the fellows should tell you, not somebody else."

Carl said he couldn't see why Bill was making such a fuss about Charles's remark because "he [the leader] could easily find out if he wanted to." Bill again repeated his observation that nobody should squeal. Charles said maybe Bill was afraid "somebody would say that about you."

Quite upset and annoyed, Bill said "I'll tell it myself." He went on to say that he understood why he got into trouble, was positive he wouldn't have the same difficulties on the outside and was positive he was ready for release. The leader said he thought it was interesting that Bill could become so upset about Charles's statement since everybody in the group knew that Pat had difficulty working and he had, in fact, told the group about it on one occasion.

All of the boys smiled, and the leader asked Pat if he thought Charles was "a squealer" because of what he had said.

Pat said he didn't feel that way and went on to say the remark "hurt me a little" but "I think Charles is my best friend." Bill said he didn't think a boy in the group should make remarks of this kind about another boy.

The leader asked the group if any of them thought the way Bill felt about things might be related to what the group is able to talk about. Carl said it could be and Frank said, "I don't think telling another guy some of his faults is squealing if you do it in here" and added, "I have trouble talking about my problems." Bill said maybe he would feel differently if "it was one of my old friends."

Carl and Bob started to kid Bill about Charles's earlier remarks, that perhaps he was afraid some of the boys might tell him some things he didn't want to hear. Bill became angry and annoyed, complained that everybody should be a "nice guy." He went on to say that if you tell people "their faults," you're not being a "pal of theirs."

The leader asked the group if they didn't think Charles was being a good friend of Pat's since he seemed to be trying to help him not only get discharged, but maybe be a little happier after his discharge. All the group members including Bill agreed but Bill said, "I don't think you should say it; the fellows should say it about himself. I'll tell you anything you want to know. I never had any troubles outside. All I did was steal. I told you why I wanted to do that; I wanted to get nice clothes but nobody in my gang steals anymore. I was the only one and now I've stopped."

Most of the boys smiled and the leader asked Carl why he was laughing. He replied, "Bill is always telling you he stopped stealing and that he is ready to go home. I don't think you believe him." Bill said he had a feeling that "you don't believe me. Sometimes when I look at you I think you would like to keep me here forever; other times I think you like me." The leader asked if anyone could think of reasons for this. Nobody replied but Bill, who said, "I guess it's the way you look at me; I don't know. Maybe it's the way you smile."

The group was silent for a few minutes. Several of the boys moved restlessly in their seats. Finally Frank said, "Here we go again."

Most of the boys laughed at this remark and the leader asked Bob if he could think of any reasons why the group has difficulties either getting started or spending the time arguing and complaining. Bob said, "I know you think I have something to do with it but that's in the past." This surprised the group and when I asked them if they had any idea what Bob was talking about, nobody replied. The leader said that perhaps what Bob wanted to say was that his strong feelings of dislike and resentment for him which Bob had never been able to talk about in the group might have some relation to the problem we were discussing. Several of the boys moved about uneasily in their seats and Bob said, "I think we got that straightened out. I wish you would say *did* and not *has* feelings of resentment. It's like I said; I resent authority." The leader said he thought all the group recognized this but since they had not been able to talk about it in the past, perhaps some members thought it was a major issue that had to be discussed before they could talk about other things.

Several of the boys, Carl, Charles, and Frank, nodded their heads in agreement and Bob said, "That was in the past." The leader suggested at the close of the hour that perhaps the group would find it easier to get started now that some of these things were out in the open and were recognized by all. Bob said, "I feel better now that it's out." The leader again pointed out that it is easier to talk about things if they are recognized and accepted by all.[4]

A unique institution and one which utilizes group approaches is the California Medical Facility, operated by the State Department of Corrections. It has the custodial and legal features of a prison, but the staff and climate of a hospital. It is a special unit for physically and mentally handicapped male adult offenders—tuberculars, psychotics, homosexuals, drug addicts, sex deviates, and a variety of others. The sex offenders have been transferred here either from a Reception-Guidance Center or from one of the other prisons of the state.

The aggressive sex offenders receive individual psycho-

[4] Lloyd W. McCorkle, "Group Therapy in the Treatment of Offenders," *Federal Probation*, XVI, No. 4 (1952), 22–27.

therapy, "but the method of choice is group psychotherapy which has been expanded to such an extent as to embrace almost all the patients." [5]

The group program is conducted by trained therapists, with an average of ten patients per worker, a gratifyingly low ratio making effective relationships possible and probable. Patients —they are called that, and not "prisoners"—attend two group meetings a week. "The therapist assumes a dominant but unobtrusive role. Patients are encouraged to express their feelings freely, to expose their problems, and with the aid of the group to understand themselves." There are distress and hostility at the outset, but gradually "members of the group begin to bring their submerged feelings to the surface. Conflicts are slowly resolved, tensions decreased, and energies redirected." [6] The Director of the Department of Corrections, Richard A. McGee, reports that change for the better occurs often enough "to justify the conclusion that group psychotherapy is the most effective approach today." [7]

New Jersey and several other states are experimenting with group techniques. They give promise of providing an economical and at the same time highly beneficial treatment program.

[5] State of California, Department of Corrections, *1955–56 Biennial Report*, p. 38.
    [6] *Ibid.*   [7] *Ibid.,* p. 39.

13

RULES AND REGULATIONS

We want to help people. The rules and regulations applying to probationers and parolees are meant to facilitate the helping process. Are these prescriptions and proscriptions sound?

Rules and regulations are authoritative, but we have seen that authority, per se, does not vitiate an effective casework relationship. If both the officer and the person under supervision can keep clearly in mind the functions of the agency, the purposes of the service, then rules and regulations can be viewed in proper perspective. The functions and limits of the correctional agency define what shall be the rules and regulations. The statement of those rules clarifies for probationer or parolee what those functions and limits are, what the officer is there to do, what is expected of the individual under supervision, and how he can get help from the organization.

A statement of rules and regulations, then, has positive casework meaning. It clarifies the aims of the agency for both the officer and his charge. It lays the foundation for treatment by establishing the ground rules.

Caseworkers in other types of agency would agree with this. They would say that casework in any organization is actually impossible without some rules. The relief client must meet eligibility requirements. Individuals seeking help with regard to emotional problems undertake to come to the family service agency at certain hours. They must give themselves to the painful business of discussing intimate details of their lives, else treatment cannot be attempted. There are two reasons why rules must play a part in casework. First, they have a practical administrative function. Public assistance laws must be complied with in a relief agency. A probation or parole officer is charged by law with law enforcement responsibilities. A second reason for regulations is psychological. All of us are more comfortable when we "know the rules." Rules establish the limits. They underscore the reality situation—how far we can go and still be approved. Children thrive under intelligent discipline which indicates, "You may walk up to this line, but if you step over it, you will be punished." That makes them freer to get as far as the line without insecurity. Some adults find personal security in the strict regimentation of military service. Probationers and parolees may not always be consciously aware of the fact, but there is emotional security to be derived from knowing, "so far I can go, but no further."

Rules and regulations, we have said, are intended for the ex-offender's benefit every bit as much as for the welfare of the community. To accomplish this double objective, they must be used constructively. We might posit certain generalizations on this score:

1. Rules and regulations need to be applied on an individualized basis so far as possible. That is, they are most useful when adapted to the needs of the given individuals and conditions. A blanket rule that all probationers must refrain from committing further crime is sound enough, so much a foregone conclusion as to be almost banal. But John might be enjoined from drinking while Sam is allowed more leeway, yet both do well on probation or parole.

2. Psychologically, the positive approach is to be preferred in the wording of regulations. Consider for a moment how you would feel if someone said, "You must not drive a car." It ls; it hurts; it seems unfair. Now suppose you were told, ay drive a car. To qualify, you will need to pass a test." g has gone out of it, hasn't it? The second statement

sounds less forbidding than the first? That is because it begins
with a "yes" and not a "no." It tells you how to get an official
nod rather than a traffic ticket.

The printed rules and regulations handed a probationer or
parolee would probably be more favorably received and understood if expressed in "yes" rather than "no" language. Instead,
the majority speak in "Thou shalt nots."

The United States Board of Parole has made one of the few
attempts to couch rules in positive terms. Its printed statement
issued to parolees and conditional releasees does not say: "You
must not change your employment without permission." Instead, the little brochure asserts, "If you wish to secure a new
job . . . you must make application to your Probation Officer."
That, at least, is less formidable in connotation. Another section of the brochure states:

Your Adviser and Probation Officer wish you to succeed on parole
and are willing to stand behind you if you are trying to do what
is right and abiding by parole regulations. If you need help let
them know. Do not conceal your troubles from them. If you get
into difficulty, tell your Adviser and your Probation Officer about
it at once.[1]

Some agencies would begin with the last sentence and end
there.

3. We should not enjoin unless we mean to enforce. If we
say the former offender must not take even one drink, we must
be prepared to exact a penalty every time he does. If we do
not mean to do so, we ought not to make the rule so positive
and rigid. To establish a rule then allow it to be violated with
impunity makes the regulation meaningless and invites con-
tempt of all regulations.

4. Rules and regulations should be sensible, reasonable,
workable. They should have a logic.

[1] In the Federal system, probation officers are really probation and parole
officers. They handle both types of case.

A Federal judge placed a defendant on probation for mail embezzlement. When the probationer, who weighed 240 pounds, indicated he intended to get a bricklaying job, the jurist allegedly said, "You're too fat to be climbing around scaffolding. As part of your probation I order you to take off fifty pounds." [2]

There are several counts against this order. The instruction is perhaps unworkable, for we know that extreme overweight is often a neurotic symptom, and even the order of an awe-inspiring jurist will not wipe out a neurosis. Further, it may be dangerous for the man to take off fifty pounds. Moreover, the provision is not directly related to the defendant's criminal behavior, hence it lacks a logic for him. It may confuse his understanding of the function of probation. What does that have to do with his avoirdupois?

Conditions of Probation and Parole

Let us examine rules and regulations found in probation and parole.

1. *Paying costs of the court action.*—This condition is only occasionally imposed in probation cases and not at all in parole. Many people in the field consider the requirement unsound because it is unrelated to any known recidivism factor. A person who is going to do well on probation, they assert, will do so whether or not he pays court costs. And those who cannot afford to pay are discriminated against when ordered to do so.

Others in the field believe the stipulation has a salutary effect in selected cases, impressing upon them in tangible fashion that illegal behavior brings financially painful consequences. ꞏourage contrition, strike at the offender's pocketbook, ꞏgest.

ꞏy, the issue is of no great consequence. Only a frac-

Times, August 8, 1955.

tion of potential probationers are involved. And most judges take into account ability to pay. They will not impose the condition on an individual who cannot afford to comply.

2. *Paying a fine as a condition of liberty.*—This stipulation, when it appears, is also restricted to probation. It is not the same as a fine added to a penal sentence. In the latter instance, the fine is part of the adjudication and must be paid or additional time served. A fine as a condition of probation is imposed upon defendants otherwise deemed fit risks.

Here again, opinion is divided as to the efficacy of such a stipulation. Some believe it serves no practical purpose, while others hold that it impresses an offender who might otherwise feel he is "getting away with something" if granted probation with no financial strings attached.

3. *Serving a jail term as a condition of probation.*—As indicated, this is found in probation cases only. As a condition, the judge orders the defendant to serve a specified period in jail before coming under supervision in the free community. While incarcerated, the offender is technically a probationer and the time spent under incarceration is credited against total period to be served on probation.

While some penologists insist this serves the purpose, again, of demonstrating that the probationer "isn't getting away with it," the preponderance of opinion is opposed to this practice. Most correctional workers who have expressed themselves on the subject hold this stipulation is a violation of the spirit of probation. If, they ask, the judge feels the defendant is a safe risk for probation, why does he incarcerate him? If he feels he is not a safe risk, why does he offer him probation at all? Furthermore, these people say, a stay in an institution, particularly a muncipal or county jail, subjects the defendant to influences which more often than not make him worse, not better, upon release. Is this what the judge wants? Is this an objective of probation?

The Standard Probation and Parole Act, sponsored by the National Probation and Parole Association, declares: "The practice . . . is a contradiction in terms and in concept and is condemned. The purpose of probation is to avoid, where it is feasible, the impact of institutional life."

Fortunately, few states follow this procedure, and where it is accepted practice, the percentage of cases in which it is applied is quite low, probably less than 5 percent of the total number of defendants placed on probation.

4. *Making restitution.*—Often in probation, less frequently in parole, the offender is ordered to make monetary restitution to the person or persons victimized. Common sense dictates that such repayment, when ordered, shall be made when the individual is earning enough to comply. Installment payments are the general rule.

In their annual reports, many probation departments make much of the dollars collected in restitution. The large sums repaid to victims are often cited as one argument for the use of probation.

There would seem to be sound reasons for the stipulation in given cases. It is not only that aggrieved persons are recompensed. Unlike a fine as a condition of probation, or service of a jail term prior to supervision, restitution has an understandable logic. It is directly related to the offense and the attitude of the offender. There is a reality involved: society does not sanction fraud or other forms of theft; it does not approve injury inflicted upon an innocent person. Society wants to make sure the offender realizes the enormity of his conduct, and it asks him to demonstrate this by making amends to the individual most affected by the defendant's depredations.

There is nothing prejudicial about this. When the law-abiding individual borrows money, he must repay. If he accidentally injures another, civil law may require him to pay medical bills and perhaps for loss of working time and capacity.

Restitution may have a positive casework connotation. It offers the individual something within reason that he can do here and now, within the limits of his ability, to demonstrate to *himself* that he is changing. A fine is punitive. A jail sentence is retributive. But restitution makes sense. It is every man's obligation to meet responsibilities of this sort in civil life.

To be sure, casework considerations may indicate that restitution should *not* be ordered. It is no magic formula. The backgrounds and needs of the individual case should determine whether or not the stipulation is to be laid down. The mark of effective probation and parole surely is not how much money has been collected, nor even how helpful restitution is to the injured parties, but how effectively it is used as a tool in treatment toward the end that the offender shall not offend again.

5. *Paying for supervision.*—Michigan statutes carry a curious provision. The court may charge a defendant with "all such expenses, direct and indirect, as the public has been or may be put to in connection with the apprehension, examination, trial and probationary oversight of the probationer." A probation condition may be that the person under supervision pay the cost of such treatment. The practice of charging probationers still exists, although it has fallen off considerably in recent years. Currently, some ten or twelve of Michigan's eighty-three counties make such charges. The fees usually are in the amount of two dollars a month. The monies are turned over to the general fund of the county.[3]

To the present writer this regulation is an anachronism, somewhat on the order of a Pennsylvania ordinance which provides that an individual arrested by the police shall pay five dollars for his ride in the police wagon. Suppose he declines the honor of riding? Will he be set free? Suppose the probationer fails to pay the fee? Will he be locked up just for that? Monies are

[3] Letter to the author by Harold Kachelski, Research Analyst, State of Michigan Department of Corrections, July 18, 1958.

appropriated for correctional services. If a defendant is considered fit material for probation, should he not receive it,
at government expense, in the interest of society every bit as
much as of the probationer? Actually, the probationer is already
taxed, along with the rest of us, for the service. He pays sales
and income taxes. He might well declare, as we all so often
do, "I'm entitled to this service! I'm a taxpayer!"

While the majority of fieldworkers disparage the practice
of charging fees for probation service, it is just conceivable
that such a scheme, differently oriented, may someday come
to serve a useful purpose. In recent decades it has become an
increasing practice in private casework agencies to charge a
modest fee of clients. Caseworkers believe this helps the client
maintain his self-respect—he is paying for what he gets. Moreover, by paying, he is focusing on the fact that he wants something of this agency, and is ready to do what he can to get
the most out of this service for which he is paying. Perhaps
fee-charging can serve a like purpose in probation—and in
parole, too—if it can be invested with this meaning. Fee-charging might establish itself as a significant coadjuvant in the
process of clarifying agency function for probationers and parolees. It would have to be graduated on the basis of ability
to pay, of course. And there would always be a few probationers and parolees unable, due to intellectual incapacity, to
understand agency function whether or not they are in a fee-
charging relationship. It would serve no purpose to have them
pay.

6. *Making an arrival report.*—Persons placed on probation
are conducted from court to the probation office, where the
supervising officer meets his new charge. Parolees are generally
required to report to the officer as soon after release from the
institution as possible.

A parolee's failure to make an arrival report is a danger

signal. He travels from the institution to the office without escort. If he fails to show up, it may well signify he never intended to place himself under supervision. Or it may mean that en route he stopped off at a bar; the removal of restraint was too much for him; he became drunk and will need drying out before further plans for his future can be considered.

7. *Reporting.*—Practically every probation and parole system requires reports from the former offender at specified intervals. Unfortunately, this does not invariably mean to the office, in person. Mailed reports are sometimes permitted. This might mean a letter from the probationer or parolee in which he gives certain required minimal information. Such letters are apt to be sterile and meaningless. One parolee, for instance, sent in several hundred letters in the course of a lengthy supervision period, each giving only name, address, employment, and the comment: "I have no problems to discuss." The gentleman so fortunate as to have no problems of any moment was eventually shot dead in a gang war.

Sometimes mailed reports take the form of completed questionnaires indicating residence, employment, recreational activities, budget, savings, and other items. A questionnaire assures that certain needed information is provided, but a ten-inch blank provided for answers to questions is scarcely conducive to eliciting data regarding marital difficulties, emotional conflicts, anxieties, fears, ambitions, plans for the future.

Some workers hold that any kind of reporting, whether in person or by mail, is a futile process, yielding unverified, nonspontaneous information. Even in personal interviews, due to pressures of time, the officer is likely to rap out questions, the probationer or parolee answering in an inhibiting atmosphere laden with tensions. Asked, "Are you still working?" the individual may reply easily enough. But should the worker ask, "Are you and your wife getting along better?" the very at-

mosphere of the reporting station may produce a "Yes," just
to get it over with, even if "I should say not!" would be the
appropriate answer.

There is no question that in most organizations conditions
for office reporting are far from ideal. Nevertheless, reporting
would seem to serve a purpose. It is not intended as a base
for casework interviewing. Where this is indicated, it is accomplished much better by special appointment, at the erstwhile offender's home, or in the office, under circumstances
providing privacy and a minimum of tension. Official reports
are not expected to be the same as casework interviews, although in many agencies they must serve the double purpose,
due to time limitations and excessive caseloads. Where this
is so, they are bound to be limited in effectiveness. But the primary aim of the official report is community protection. It is
here we get the starting point for casework treatment and field
investigation. The officer must know that the probationer or
parolee is alive and available on at least the given day and hour.
He must get from him certain basic information: where he lives
and works, what is happening in his family, and what he does
in his spare time. According to the report, such and such are
the facts.

Of course, anyone who has worked in the field is keenly
aware that office reports frequently yield something less than
the complete truth. It is improbable that such an overwhelm-
ing proportion as so report spend their leisure time in taking
a walk, watching television, or settling into bed with a good
book. Through duplicity, those under supervision hope to avoid
unpleasantness. They are not going to admit they committed
crime, if they did. They will be untruthful about certain lesser
matters. But their very evasions and untruths have meaning,
and it is important to uncover that meaning. When the officer,
armed with what the probationer or parolee says are the facts,
goes into the field and finds discrepancies, he has come upon

something usually highly significant. Then he begins his job of protecting the community or helping the former offender work his way out of some troubling situation.

Sally J. reported to her parole officer that she continued to live with her husband and two children at 544 Zenith Street. Mr. J., she said, was earning $125 a week and supporting the family adequately. Sally asserted she spent her time in caring for the household and, in her spare time, acting as Den Mother for a Cub Scout group. She expressed herself as happy in her home life, but the officer sensed some unrest within her. Further queries, however, elicited nothing beyond what had already been averred.

The officer called at 544 Zenith Street and discovered the J. family had moved two weeks before. The superintendent of the apartment house said she understood the family had broken up, Mrs. J. taking the children.

Further investigation included visits to relatives of the couple, but no lead as to the whereabouts of the parolee were turned up. A check with the utilities company, however, revealed a new address for Mrs. J. The officer made inquiries there, found the parolee was living in a small apartment with her children. She was working. The oldest daughter took care of the younger child during the day.

The following week, when Sally reported, she was not aware the officer had this information. Faced with the fact, she burst into tears, apologizing, "I shouldn't have lied to you!" She admitted she and her husband had not found themselves congenial since the parolee returned from the reformatory. Mr. J. could not forgive her for the manner in which she had disgraced the family. He quarreled over the rearing of the children, repeatedly sneering that Sally was scarcely a person to know how to raise youngsters decently.

Sobbing, Sally told the officer she had taken as much as she could, then moved out, because, "I was ashamed to have the kids hear all that." She did love her children, she cried, and she insisted she was a good mother, no matter what her husband thought. She had not reported what was going on in the household because, "I was ashamed."

Sally had lied to her parole officer. She had violated rules by moving without notification. But she showed a sense of responsibility for the children. She worked. She was making an adequate home for her brood. The spurious office reports had merely opened the way to casework service, not to revocation of parole. Sally was continued under supervision, the officer helping her adjust to her changed circumstances thereafter.

But in another case:

Sibyl T., unmarried, on parole for forgery, formerly a prostitute, reported she was living at 327 Wildwood Avenue, with her aged mother. She asserted she was employed at the Sunrise Trucking Company as a clerk in the downtown office. She exhibited a pay envelope, with her name typed on it, along with notations regarding deductions for Social Security.

Sibyl spoke with pride of the fact she had never had confidence, before, in her ability to hold a job of this sort. She described her work, and how happy she was in it. Her employer, she said, was highly satisfied, and promised her a raise in the near future.

Mrs. Gibson, the parole officer, called at the alleged place of employment, only to discover that Sibyl never worked there. Moreover, the firm paid by check, not by pay envelope.

The officer proceeded to the home of Sibyl's mother. Mrs. T. upbraided the parolee, calling her "a tramp all over again," saying she had been running around with a very bad crowd.

Further investigation disclosed Sibyl had met a man who turned out to be a procurer. He put her in business as a prostitute. It was he who furnished the "pay envelope" for purposes of deception.

Here, the official report led to disclosures which called for activity quite different from that in the case of Sally J. The parolee was apprehended and returned to the institution.

Reporting, then, is a starting point for indicated casework and community protection. It can also constitute a salutary discipline if used constructively. It gives the probationer or parolee an opportunity to do certain things, take affirmative steps in maintaining his good standing. He assumes the responsibility of reporting, where and when required. He has the obligation of telling the truth. To that extent, he is participating in the treatment process. It is a simple duty, for the most part, not too onerous if one is behaving properly.

That reports do act as a control on the individual is suggested by this writer's field experience. It was a matter of note that, too often to be mere chance, when a parolee who had been reporting weekly had his status relaxed to a monthly basis, he got into trouble immediately thereafter, as if the lessening of restraint was too much for him.

Helen M. Kelleher reported on the case of Mrs. Beckman,[4] a near-prostitute under instructions to report weekly to the caseworker, who acted as a semiofficial arm of the probation system in this instance. About three months after the initial contact, Mrs. Beckman was informed she could report monthly thereafter. That same night she was arrested for disorderly conduct and "leading a lewd and dissolute course of life."

Experiences like these suggest that reporting has meaning as a device for strengthening self-control. They also indicate that a problem still to be studied is how best to relax reporting status, and when.

8. *Keeping the officer informed of whereabouts.*—This regulation scarcely requires discussion. If officers are to treat those under their jurisdiction effectively, if they are to provide community protection, they must know where their charges are living and under what conditions.

9. *Getting, keeping, and reporting honestly on employment.* —Good habits of work have a stabilizing effect upon behavior. Adults need to earn a living. The agency wants assurance that the source of income is legitimate. There is good reason, therefore, to stipulate that those who should work, seek employment, hold onto their jobs within reason, and labor only in legitimate enterprises. The same is required of any of us.

Obviously, this does not signify that a probationer or parolee must accept any legitimate employment at all, at whatever wages, under whatever conditions.

[4] Helen M. Kelleher, "The Record of Mrs. Pauline Beckman's Year of Probation," in Rosa Wessel, ed., *A Casework Approach to Sex Delinquents* (Philadelphia: Pennsylvania School of Social Work, 1947), pp. 88–125.

A former light opera tenor was on probation for family desertion. His officer instructed him to seek work, since nothing in his chosen field was available. When the probationer was unable to locate a job, the worker found one for him, and told him he expected him to begin the next day.

The probationer became almost hysterical at the prospect. He could not possibly be a clerk in a business establishment, he cried. If permitted to wait only a few weeks, two months at the most, the light opera season would have opened and he would find something. He did not believe he should be forced to accept work for which he was temperamentally unsuited.

Since the probationer had no reserve funds, the officer felt he should take the proffered position for the few weeks. But since doing so would apparently create such an emotional upheaval, he wanted to be fair. He offered the probationer the opportunity to present his arguments to the Senior Probation Officer.

In a three-way conference, it was finally agreed that provided the probationer got a loan from his union, as he believed he could, he would not be expected to take the clerical post.

He did secure the loan, which tided him over until he was able to get back into theatrical work.

Sensible procedure also precludes attempting to force probationers or parolees to work in struck plants. They should not be penalized if, as union men, they go out on a strike called by union officials. The fact that they are on probation does not justify depriving them of a right they would have under other circumstances. Revocation of civil rights, if it took place, did not include this disprivilege.

Nor should the fact an individual is on probation or parole serve as justification for directing him to accept work at a salary lower than others are receiving for the same operation. His status should not force him to take work under conditions less favorable than those of employees who do not have records. The employer pays on the basis of capacity. He is not entitled to reduce an employee's market value because of prior record in crime, in the estimation of the majority of penologists who have expressed themselves on this subject.

When a man is legitimately employed, he has no reason to be untruthful about it. Untruthful reports naturally lead to the suspicion there may be an illicit source of income or that the person concerned is lazy. Trouble is afoot if a probationer or parolee claims to be working when he is not; if he plays all night and cannot get up in the morning to seek or hold employment; if he drifts from job to job; if he has no visible means of support. Some people do not work because they have neurotic traits which incapacitate them psychologically. That concerns the officer at one level. Other men and women will not work at legitimate employment because they are involved in illegal enterprise. That concerns the officer at another level.

10. *Supporting dependents.*—We all have this obligation. Should the probationer or parolee be an exception?

11. *Avoiding indebtedness and unreasonable expenditures.* —The intent of this rule is clear. We want to encourage thrift, sensible budgeting, responsible habits. But how are we going to define what is and what is not a reasonable expenditure? Buying a Cadillac is unreasonable in the case of a man earning $100 a week and with no money in the bank. It is quite reasonable in the instance of a highly paid executive. Individualization must be the rule.

Scarcely anybody goes through life without incurring some indebtedness. When is it advisable and when not? The officer has an obligation to interpret for the particular case. No formula will serve for all.

A parolee asked permission to buy a car "on time." His request was approved, since he required a motor vehicle in connection with his employment, and earned enough to make installment payments. Another parolee wanted to refurnish his home. It would cost about $2,500, of which $2,000 would be paid in installments. The parolee had a sporadic work record. The officer advised against going into debt. The parolee did not buy the furniture.

But suppose, despite the guidance of his officer, the man had determined he would go into debt for furniture? Would the officer have been justified in ordering him to desist? By virtue of rules and regulations, yes. But the question points up another consideration. There are benefits to be derived from allowing people to do their own budgeting, make their own decisions regarding expenditures. They will make mistakes, but how will they learn to handle money sensibly if they are not given the opportunity to make decisions regarding its use? Relief agencies more and more give assistance in cash rather than in kind. They place upon families the onus of so handling the grant that it will last through the stipulated period. The purpose is to inculcate a spirit of responsibility in such matters, and this requires that the client have the right to make decisions.

Something akin to this seems appropriate in probation and parole. Officers have a responsibility to guide those who need help in learning to handle money. This would be particularly so with juveniles. Workers have an obligation to protect dependents of probationers and parolees against extravagances which would leave them without the necessities of life. It is the function of officers to look into questionable expenditures when there is any suspicion they may in some manner be related to conduct which might lead to serious violation of probation or parole. Beyond this, how far need we go?

An officer wants to consider carefully before taking from a human being the right to self-determination, the authority to act like a grownup person with responsibilities. He would not want to emulate the probation officer who told a man under his supervision he should stop eating meat and substitute fish, because meat was more expensive and cut into his budget too heavily. The probationer said he hated fish and so did his entire family; he needed meat to keep him going at his heavy laboring job. But the officer was adamant. Meat cost twice as much as fish and would have to go. It would seem the probationer should have had the right to determine his family's diet in a situation of this sort. To refuse him that right was to place him in the position of a child. Certainly the denial did nothing to further his emotional maturity or ability to solve his problems independently.

12. *Requiring the person under care to submit to medical or psychiatric care.*—This requirement, found fairly frequently, calls for interpretation. Any individual may be required to have medical treatment if he is infected with a communicable disease. Public health laws so provide. Making it a regulation of probation or parole amounts to a duplication, although it would seem to do no harm.

Psychiatric care is another matter. If a person be psychotic the law provides for him. Whether he agrees or not, he will be hospitalized. But the neurotic, the psychopath, is not covered in law. It would appear that while he may be led to the psychiatrist, he cannot be forced to give himself to treatment. To profit from treatment, psychiatrists say, it is necessary that the patient come willingly. It serves little purpose, therefore, to order a probationer or parolee to go for treatment when he does not want to do so. The officer does better if he tries to interpret to the individual that he needs that sort of help—if he does. And, let us confess, sometimes he does not, even when efforts are made to put him on the psychiatrist's couch. It seems to this writer that, on occasion, those in authority—officer, judge, parole board member—are too quick to consider psychiatry. To some it may appear to have magical qualities. They feel better if they know the person under care will receive this magical treatment. Perhaps this is because of the understandable frustration occasioned by the realization that other techniques are not effective. The motivation for requiring such therapy is sound enough, but if results will be nil, is it worth while making the stipulation?

Henry ran breathlessly into a police station to report a lion had escaped from a cage and was ranging the highways and byways of the city. He owned the animal, a feature of his carnival act.

The city was alerted. In one evening, the lion was reported in a dozen different places at the same time. He was spotted in woods and on the streets. He jumped out at motorists, chased children, and roared outside dwellings. Police dashed madly over the terrain, and when they never did lay eyes on the elusive animal, they began to wonder. Investigation disclosed the lion did exist, but he was reposing in his cage, which had been removed to a hiding place. Henry admitted he had perpetrated a hoax.

He was arrested, eventually placed on probation. The judge imposed a special condition: Henry must take psychiatric treatment.

Henry demurred, asserting there was nothing wrong with him that a job wouldn't cure. He perpetrated the hoax, he declared, to demonstrate what a fine publicity man he could be. He was angling for such a post with a circus, thought he'd pull a spectacular caper and prove his worth. He was no more, and no less, unbalanced than any other publicity man, Henry declared, but if the only way he'd make probation was to agree to treatment, he would agree.

He did visit the psychiatrist once. Nothing happened. Nothing could happen; for Henry recognized no problem within himself requiring treatment, and probably there was none. He decided not to go back a second time. He assumed this would constitute him a probation violator, and he absconded.

He was apprehended and ordered to begin service of the suspended prison term. Had the special condition of probation not been imposed, it is very likely Henry would have made a "successful" probationer.

Ordering psychiatric treatment is akin to the practice of a certain judge who "sentences" defendants to attend church. If a man has to be sentenced to attend church, chances are he is not in a frame of mind to do so, and the "sentence" will not change his mind. If a person must be ordered to seek psychiatric treatment, chances are he is not ready for it, even if he needs it.

13. *Remaining within the jurisdiction.*—Regulations usually provide that the person concerned is not to leave the jurisdic-

tion without permission. In probation, the county is likely to be the unit of jurisdiction. In a state parole system the state line defines the boundaries. The reason for the rule is clear. The organization is authorized to maintain authority over its charges only within its precincts. Jurisdiction would not extend beyond those limits. Where there is sufficient reason, a temporary visit to another jurisdiction can be arranged. Should it seem desirable to allow a permanent move to another area, this too is possible. By prearrangement, supervision would be assumed by the receiving state or county for the sending agency. Reports would be furnished the latter, which would retain legal control over the status of the probationer or parolee. But when there is no reason for the individual to be out of the original jurisdiction, the agency responsible for his supervision wants him within reach.

14. *Owning and operating an automobile.*—The majority of probation and parole systems have a rule providing that a person under supervision shall not drive a motor vehicle without a license and specific permission from the agency to have that license. Juveniles below driving age are not, of course, given such permission.

The regulation is intended to prevent the use of vehicles for illicit purposes. Some individuals would be dangerous behind the wheel because they have a proclivity for drunken driving. Others have in the past committed offenses in which a car was used. To be sure, a person bent on crime or delinquency might not hesitate to drive a car without permission, if he felt he needed it in the commission of the offense. On the other hand, there are many cases where *because* they are bent on such an offense the perpetrators make sure they do have a valid license. Should they get away from the scene of the crime successfully and then happen to violate some traffic ordinance, they do not want to be subject to the close questioning that would ensue if they were stopped by police and unable to produce a license.

In any event, there is no reason why the probation or parole agency should not try to control the situation as far as possible by requiring prior approval for the issuance of a license.

The agencies are quite willing to concede that many former offenders live in areas in which a car is essential for transportation to and from work. It is recognized, too, that a car, in proper hands, is an acceptable source of recreation for the family. Where an automobile is presumably needed, for work or social reasons, the agency asks only that it have the right to determine whether a driver's license should be approved. If so, it wants to make sure the license is secured without fraud based upon withholding information concerning a court record.

15. *Possessing other licenses.*—This regulation applies particularly in states that grant a combined hunting and fishing license. There probably would be no strictures against fishing, but hunting implies the use of firearms. Agencies do not take the position that they will never grant permission for a hunting license to be issued to a probationer or parolee. They merely want to control who shall and shall not have the right to carry weapons. This would be decided on an individual basis, in the public interest.

16. *Abstaining from the use or overuse of intoxicants.*—This provision is found in almost every jurisdiction. For instance, the use of alcoholic beverages by a parolee is completely prohibited by parole agencies in forty-one states. It is permitted, but not to excess, in four states.

Undoubtedly, some restriction is desirable in given cases. However, a blanket regulation applied to all under supervision presents difficulties. Probably no one questions that juveniles should be held strictly to the no-drinking stipulation. But where adults are concerned, a number of facts should be considered:

1. Liquor affects people differently. Some go wild, some become lachrymose, some comatose.

2. A dosage intoxicating to one man leaves another cold sober.

3. Some people can drink and know when to stop. Others, after the first swallow, are bound to have the second and third and fourth, and wind up in serious trouble.

4. We do not have much valid information on the part drinking plays in delinquency and crime, despite many positive assertions on the subject.

In the light of these considerations, a blanket regulation seems unnecessary and unduly restrictive. If we say, "You must not drink," we obligate ourselves to assess a penalty upon every violation of the proscription, and that would be unjust in many cases.

Why should not the regulation read something like this: "Your probation (parole) officer will tell you what rule applies in your case regarding the use of alcoholic beverages"? Then the worker could tell one man or woman, in effect, "It is clear from your history that after one drink you are dangerous. Therefore, you must not take that drink. If you do, we shall be forced to arrest you." A second person might be told: "You handle yourself pretty well. We will not prohibit your taking a drink, even several drinks. But you must accept the responsibility of not imbibing to the point where you are in danger of getting yourself or others into trouble."

Members of Alcoholics Anonymous say they are not against drinking, that if a person can drink without harming himself or others, that is fine. The A.A. member envies him. He only says that he is an alcoholic, with no tolerance for liquor; hence he must never touch a drop, for he would be bound to take another and would get into difficulties. This viewpoint is adaptable to probation and parole. Those who can drink sensibly might be given more leeway than those who cannot.

17. *Abstaining from the use of narcotics.*—It cannot be said

of the narcotics user that he can use drugs without damaging himself or others. He is almost certain to be "hooked," and addiction will destroy him, physically and mentally. A proscription may not prevent a person from using narcotics, but there is no reason why the supervising organization should not try to protect the probationer or parolee.

Better than proscription, of course, is preventive treatment. We know that practically every approach—medical, psychiatric, religious—has been relatively ineffectual in producing real and permanent cessation of drug use. One of the most hopeful approaches is well worth looking into. Narcotics Anonymous, based upon the philosophy of Alcoholics Anonymous, might be an answer to a long-felt need. If it is as successful as A.A. it certainly offers a most effective medium for preventive measures. Physicians, and penologists look with respect upon this organization.

Probation and parole, in the estimation of at least this writer, ought to welcome the possibility of working with Narcotics Anonymous. The author has sat in on many meetings of this organization. He has met men, women, and youngsters who have stopped using drugs, after many failures in the past. There are members who have remained "clean" for a decade. While no statistics are available to measure results and compare them with those produced by other methods, the fact remains that if even a few individuals are helped, the effort is well worth while.

18. *Avoiding disreputable places and associates.*—If a person frequents disreputable neighborhoods and hangouts, he is likely to meet disreputable people. They may lead him into delinquency and crime. Many a juvenile escapade and more serious forays are germinated where young people gather with no prior notion of engaging in delinquency. Says a sixteen-year-old boy, as tape recorded by the writer:

We don't just say, like, "Let's meet tomorrow night at 9 o'clock and go out and steal hubcaps or roll drunks." Things like that just happen. We'll be sitting in a drive-in, having a hamburger, and somebody will say, "Jeez, I feel bored! There ain't a goddamned thing to do in this town." Then somebody else will say, "Let's go to a show." The other fellow will say, "Nah! I seen it already. Let's go steal some hubcaps." And that's how it starts.

The injunction to avoid disreputable neighborhoods must be leavened with common sense; for it goes without saying that many offenders grow up in such areas and cannot escape them. They cannot afford to live elsewhere. Indeed, a great many no longer feel at home in a better neighborhood. They drift back to familiar haunts. Sometimes they do not get into difficulties thereby, but often they do. They cannot live in a vacuum, impervious to everything about them. Consequently, a reasonable compromise must be arrived at regarding companions and places of association. It will be an uneasy compromise at best, the element of risk always present. But the hope must be that since not all probationers and parolees can be transplanted, they may at least be helped to develop strength to resist the temptations of certain environments.

19. *Keeping reasonable hours.*—Persons under supervision are required to keep reasonable hours. This is particularly important in the case of juveniles. Moreover, there probably is a demonstrable relationship between hours and recidivism in the instance of many adults.

What constitutes a reasonable time to be home? Is it 10:30 P.M., which seems to be the favorite hour among the agencies? Or midnight, which runs a close second? If we believe in individualization, we shall be consistent and say there is no "reasonable" curfew applying to all.

Some probationers and parolees are accidental offenders, basically responsible people, able to order their lives successfully. They need no rule. Others, whatever their offenses, must be out at what would be odd hours for most of us. They work nights. Or they are like the former banker, a first offender on parole, who attended social functions at his country club. No one was harmed when he stayed out until 2 A.M. and then was chauffeured home.

But some persons under supervision do constitute question-able risks, and have no particularly valid reason to be out until the wee hours of the morning. If on the street late at night, even though for no illicit purpose, they would be subject to suspicion on the part of the police. It is to their best interests to be home by a reasonable hour, whatever that is.

A sound procedure with adults might be to stipulate curfew, if any, on an individual basis. The regulation might read: "Your officer will talk to you about hours. He will tell you by what general rule you should be guided."

For various reasons, a more formal regulation of the hours of juveniles may be justified. Some cities have curfew laws that apply to everyone in the category. Juveniles attending school ought to have the rest they need. Parents should be able to en-force any rule about hours, but many whose children are on probation and parole cannot or do not care to do so. The agency has some obligation here, it would seem.

20. *Refraining from making speeches or writing for public consumption without permission.*—Only a few agencies so stipulate. They hope to forestall derogatory and untruthful al-legations. Ex-offenders have, indeed, published articles and books heaping unjustified contumely upon public officials, penologists, parole, probation, prisons. They have been vitu-perative in public addresses. Nevertheless, it is suggested we should tread gingerly in this area of regulation. Former of-fenders have suffered some disprivilege by the loss of certain civil rights. But it is commonly conceived that they retain other, constitutional privileges, one of these being the right of free speech. If their writings or utterances violate the law, the law can penalize them, for slander or libel. Need an organiza-tion demand more protection? Cannot the agency or official

vilified defend himself adequately in the same media of communication, if he deems the attack worthy of attention? Cannot good public relations techniques build up such public understanding that unjustifiable assertions fall on deaf ears?

21. *Notifying of arrest or questioning by law-enforcement officers.*—The arrest of a probationer or parolee is of vital concern to the supervising organization. So is police questioning, whatever the outcome.

22. *Marrying without permission.*—This regulation is certainly important in the supervision of juveniles, for they may not legally marry without parental consent. Moreover, they are more likely than adults to contract "quickie" marriages which later prove bad for both parties.

What about adults on probation and parole? Should something as personal as the love relationship be regulated? Thirty-three states say "yes," speaking for parole. The argument is that marriage is regulated for all members of a society. Minors, the insane and feeble-minded, the venereally infected, have strictures placed upon their desire to marry. Many states require that all persons desirous of marrying comply with laws requiring health examinations and waiting periods. Why, then, ask some, should not persons who have been in conflict with the law be especially regulated?

Others argue that such regulation "is an unreasonable and unwarranted restriction. Moreover, it is more likely to lead to immorality than to rehabilitation. There is no justification for it. It disparages the dignity of man." [5]

The present writer takes the following position, although fully aware that not all would agree with him:

A regulation such as that under discussion has sound administrative objectives:

a) It seeks to prevent a venereally diseased person from in-

---

[5] Alexander Holtzoff, "Duties and Rights of Probationers," *Federal Probation,* XXI, No. 4 (1957), 7.

fecting the spouse, where the law does not already provide such protection.

b) It attempts to forestall fraud. If the probationer or parolee fails to divulge his or her record prior to marriage, that fact alone could justify annulment.

c) It provides time to interpose argument and a cooling-off period when immature individuals conclude in haste that they will take a chance on not repenting at leisure.

d) It gives proper weight to such factors as the feeble-mindedness of one or both parties, or the recurring insanity of one or the other member of the couple.

e) It furnishes opportunity for the officer to counsel his charge regarding such practicalities as the need to have the wherewithal to support a family.

f) It is designed to prevent illegal marriages when one or the other of the people concerned is not legally free to contract marriage.

These, it seems, are sound reasons for requiring advance approval of marriage. Beyond that, a caseworker would scarcely want to go, when an adult is concerned. Counseling is one thing; if despite that, the parties wish to marry, the right to self-determination would be seen as the guiding principle, even if indications were the marriage would not be a happy one. Many marriages in the general population are not successful. The officer is not God. He cannot be certain his prognostication is more trustworthy than the ex-offender's. Even if he felt it was (as well it might be), it is the person under care who is getting married, not the officer; and there are few things as important to an individual as the right to decide whom he will wed.

23. *Living in a meretricious relationship.*—This one is full of cockleburs. Laws against adultery and common-law relationships make it necessary that the correctional organization forbid violation lest it become party to an offense. It is inescapable,

however, that laws alone do not forestall common-law relationships, and that, moreover, many of them are stable. Others, of course, lead to emotional conflict, even crime. (So do legal marriages.)

This author's viewpoint will meet with violent dissent in many quarters, it is only fair to warn the reader. And *contra* opinion has its rationale and common-sense validity worthy of careful consideration.

The writer believes that except in states where the law permits no option, this is an area of life in which we cannot order and forbid by blanket regulation. Sometimes it becomes necessary for officers to lay down the rule bluntly and unequivocally. At other times, they will permit the individuals concerned to make the final decisions regarding the establishment of recognized and stable relationships unblessed by legal ceremony. Where, as has been stated, the law forbids such, the officer must see that the statute is obeyed. Otherwise, he knows each case is different. One regulation will not cover all contingencies.

This problem becomes involved with moral and religious considerations. The writer is not suggesting these are unimportant. They are very important. Man must have the approval of his group and of his faith if he is to be comfortable within himself. Officers have an obligation to point this out. One's religion and ethical code are an authority in themselves, by which many probationers and parolees will be guided. But if we do not wish to blink facts, we must concede that the offender group, like the nonoffender group, contains sinners who are determined to continue sinning. Some sins are against the law, and yield penalties of the law. Others are sins which are so defined by religious tenets without appearing in the statutes. If, after considering the moral implications of his proposed act, a probationer or parolee decides to live in an unsanctioned but legal relationship, the decision would seem to be his, barring considerations of public health and safety. Even that person's pastor, who might urge, plead, and excoriate, would not, finally, actually take steps to prevent such a relationship from becoming a fact.

24. *Requiring church or Sunday school attendance.*—Very few agencies carry this stipulation. Here is a statement which has much to recommend it:

Religion can be a very vital factor in rehabilitation. . . . [But] To order a person of mature years to attend church against his will is an entirely different matter. First, such an action tends to defeat its own objective, for it is apt to make him resentful rather than religious. Second, it is a violation of the probationer's constitutional right of religious freedom. This is one of the rights that are not lost by the conviction of a crime. Freedom of religion, as guaranteed by the Constitution, comprises not only the right to worship God in one's own way, but also the right not to worship Him at all.[6]

25. *Permitting visits to home and employment.*—Such visitation is essential to supervision. The officer is charged with knowing what the individual under his care is doing, so far as can be determined. Field investigation is a *sine qua non* in the furtherance of this objective. Homes can be visited without embarrassment to occupants. Employment can be checked without causing loss of jobs.

26. *Carrying or possessing dangerous weapons.*—We discussed this in connection with regulations concerning hunting licenses. Some persons would be dangerous when in possession of weapons. We have the right to restrict their use even more stringently among probationers and parolees than among civilians without a record.

28. *Regulating juveniles.*—Most of the regulations we have discussed apply to adults and juveniles alike, although some are more pertinent than others to a given category. Additionally, certain provisions are drafted for juveniles only. Those stipulating regular school attendance would not be debated.

[6] *Ibid.*, pp. 7–8.

Neither would rules requiring obedience to parents or guardians, provided they are administered with an understanding of human nature and appreciation of the fact that no one is perfect every hour of his waking life.

More questionable is the occasional instruction that directs the individual under supervision to affiliate with a recommended recreational agency.

To sum up:

Rules and regulations are necessary.

They require adept administration, skillful individualization. Few can be applied indiscriminately to all offenders.

They are most effective when worded so as not to require immediate revocation upon the merest infraction, unless that is exactly what is intended. Ideally, regulations should be permissive legislation, as it were, authorizing but not demanding revocation under given conditions. Revocation should occur only when the subject gives indication he or she is no longer a risk in society. A man might get drunk, or drive a car without a license, yet not constitute a serious danger to society. But a man who becomes inebriated often and who, while drunk, illegally drives a car, in the company of questionable associates, is subject to very serious examination to determine whether he should be at large.

Rules and regulations ought to be casework tools so far as possible, used in the interest of society and the individual.

The tests of a regulation might well be: Does it serve a constructive social purpose? Will it be enforced if seriously breached? Does it protect society? Does it aid in treatment of the offender?

14

RESULTS IN

PROBATION AND PAROLE

Do probation and parole "work"? We do not really know. There have been many inquiries on the subject but, because of methodological or other shortcomings, few valid answers.

An excellent methodology, at least, was demonstrated by the Gluecks in their epochal *500 Criminal Careers*.[1] The Harvard research team painstakingly followed the careers of 510 men released from the Massachusetts Reformatory. Many of them had been on probation; all were exposed to institutional treatment, followed by parole. What had happened to them five to fifteen years after expiration of parole? Investigators interviewed the study group, checked personal statements against official records where possible. The stunning finding was that 80 percent of the men showed an unsuccessful outcome on parole, if the criterion of success be nonrecidivism.

The procedures of the Glueck study were better than any undertaken before or since. But the findings have limited significance for several reasons. The volume was published in 1930, but the former parolees had not been exposed to the sort of treatment just coming into use. They left the reformatory between 1911 and 1922. Their parole periods ran through the 1920s. Massachusetts did not employ professional caseworkers or other highly trained counselors in this period. In other

[1] Sheldon Glueck and Eleanor T. Glueck, *500 Criminal Careers* (New York: Alfred A. Knopf, 1930).

words, the study measured some kind of probation and parole work but not the sort just beginning to be practiced.

Similarly, the Gluecks' *Five Hundred Delinquent Women* [2] studied treatment of an earlier era in correctional care. The women involved were committed to a reformatory sometime before 1915 and up to 1923. *One Thousand Juvenile Delinquents* [3] followed up cases referred by the Boston Juvenile Court to the Judge Baker Foundation for clinical examination between 1917 and 1922.

The Gluecks' trail-blazing attracted few followers willing to be as meticulous in methodology. However, using somewhat similar techniques, Beard studied 500 cases of children placed on probation in 1924 by the Boston Juvenile Court. She followed their histories five to seven years after the probation period. [4] Speaking of treatment in the country at large, she writes: "Probation in its best sense has not even been tried." [5] For what they are worth, then, here are her findings: some 80 percent of her cases fell in the "successful" category at termination of probation. By the time of the follow-up, however, only some 50 percent of the total group continued without a record of delinquency.

In 1939 the United States Attorney General reported on an analysis of 19,256 cases of probationers whose supervision had terminated within a three-year study period. [6] No field checks were made. Reliance was placed upon records from 25 probation units in 16 states and the District of Columbia. Some 61 percent of the cases had no recorded violation during the pro-

---

[2] Sheldon Glueck and Eleanor T. Glueck, *Five Hundred Delinquent Women* (New York: Alfred A. Knopf, 1934).

[3] Sheldon Glueck and Eleanor T. Glueck, *One Thousand Juvenile Delinquents* (Cambridge, Mass.: Harvard University Press, 1934).

[4] Belle Boone Beard, *Juvenile Probation* (New York: American Book Co., 1934).

[5] *Ibid.*, p. 147.

[6] *Attorney General's Survey of Release Procedures* (Washington, D.C.: Department of Justice, 1939), II, 335, 342.

bation period. Revocation of probation had been ordered in 19 percent of the cases.

The study leaves a great deal to be desired. It investigated behavior during the probation period only. There was no follow-up beyond that. The relation between treatment and outcome was not indicated. Yet, obviously, caliber of staff and treatment methods must have run the gamut from poor to good among the many jurisdictions involved.

Coming closer to modern practice chronologically was the study of adult probationers of the Erie County Probation Department, Buffalo, New York, in 1942. Two hundred cases indicted for felony were followed up five to seven years after discharge, partly by field interviews. Seventy-two percent had no known subsequent record. Twenty-eight percent had been convicted of 107 criminal charges.[7] But the 200 cases were selected on the basis of not having violated probation while under supervision. They had been "discharged with improvement." They therefore represented a highly selective sampling. The individuals would be expected to do better than an undifferentiated group.

One of the more careful and comprehensive inquiries of recent date, by Rumney and Murphy, was published in 1952. It has the merit of recency and of emanating from one of the better probation departments (Essex County, New Jersey). An advantage over previous studies is that it uses criteria additional to conviction and probation violation as measures of success and failure.[8]

The study group consisted of 1,000 offenders placed on probation in 1937. Information concerning the probationers was secured by search of records running through 1948, eleven

[7] Reported in Charles Lionel Chute and Marjorie Bell, *Crime, Courts and Probation* (New York: Macmillan, 1956), pp. 135–36.

[8] Jay Rumney and Joseph P. Murphy, *Probation and Social Adjustment* (New Brunswick, N.J.: Rutgers University Press, 1952).

years after supervision began and in most cases eight years after it terminated. Additionally, many former probationers were interviewed personally. It was found that 73 percent were discharged from probation "with improvement." Of the 764 probationers still alive and on whose after-probation history data were obtainable, 26 percent showed "marked improvement" and 33 percent some improvement. Fifty percent had not been arrested again, while 19 percent had been arrested once and 31 percent more than once since placement on probation.

As indicated, subsequent arrest or conviction was not the sole criterion of success and failure. This has a definite logic, for social readjustment cannot be measured in those terms alone. However, the method of determining improvement or lack of it was far from precise. As to treatment involved, no one orientation or standard existed. The authors frankly recognize that personnel was not ideal and caseloads were prohibitive, so that even relatively well-trained workers could not do their best. In the adult male division, for instance, loads averaged 233 per officer.

Many other studies have been undertaken, but they are less conclusive than the few we have mentioned. None unequivocally answers the question: What treatment resulted in what outcome?

In fact, we still must answer another question: Does treatment, of whatever caliber or orientation, affect outcome? We think it does, we say it does, but we have no evidence to back us up. This is shocking, and the impact is not lessened by the realization that the casework field as a whole has done very little to study what it accomplishes.

What the probation and parole field needs is more and better research. We have an obligation to find out what we are and are not accomplishing. We will not determine this by debate, but by research of the highest order, without compromise as to quality and thoroughness. With the increasing number of trained people entering the field, it is to be hoped and expected that such a contribution will be forthcoming.

One of the finest statements on the need for research comes from Raymond F. Gould, social science analyst, National Institute of Mental Health, United States Department of Health, Education, and Welfare. He begins:

Once upon a time the children of a great country were afflicted with two plagues, one affecting a few thousand each year and the other affecting over a million a year. Both were permanently crippling in many instances, and the more prevalent one was frequently damaging to others in the community. The smaller one affected the bodies of its victims; the larger one affected their minds and behavior. . . . The smaller one was regarded as a disease, and large sums were given to the physicians and men of science . . . to find ways of preventing and treating this plague. The larger one was regarded as requiring punishment, or denunciation, or conferences, or other traditional measures, and the physicians and the men of science had a relatively minor role in dealing with this plague.[9]

The smaller plague was polio. The other, as Gould expressed it, was:

an as yet unnamed set of diseases of mind and spirit which frequently manifest themselves in what is called delinquency or lawbreaking, but are also manifested in poor academic and vocational performance, disloyalty, apathy, and difficulties of interpersonal relationships which are associated with various kinds of mental illness.[10]

The methods of science and public health, he points out, were used in dealing with polio. No polio victim was blamed for his illness. Instead, scientists went to work to find preventive and treatment methods. Very little such scientific method has been brought to bear on the second plague, and Gould suggests it is high time we attacked this problem on the same

---

[9] Raymond F. Gould, "Are We Scientific about Delinquency?" *Federal Probation*, XXI, No. 4 (1957), 16.
[10] *Ibid.*, p. 17.

plane and with the same intensity as we did polio. Everything he says about attacks on delinquency is equally applicable to problems of adult criminality and treatment in probation and parole.

We do not know, Gould continues, what true delinquency is, in any sense. And we do not know conclusively the effectiveness of any delinquency prevention or treatment method. Enough knowledge now exists to encourage scientists in the belief that the time is ripe for an all-out attack on these problems.

The time is indeed ripe for an all-out attack, on all fronts, on crime and delinquency. We must get real answers to such questions as what causes delinquency and criminality, what treatment methods are effective, what we need to do to make our efforts at prevention and treatment pay dividends in social returns. Crime and delinquency are sufficiently damaging to human beings to justify as much concentrated scientific endeavor as we employ when we fight any devastating disease.

15

NEWER DIRECTIONS IN TREATMENT

If we have not gone far in research, at least we are doing some experimental work which may give new directions to treatment.

Midway Institutions

One of the knottiest problems of penology has been what to do with, for, and about the aggressive sex offender. For several decades those concerned with care and treatment of these offenders have advocated so-called "midway" institutions, part prison, part hospital. They would retain inmates in safe custody, yet treat them as patients. The emphasis would be upon medical-psychiatric care, but the patient would not be able to sign himself out if he did not want the treatment. He would be released only if and when qualified staff certified him as cured. Under such a system, some patients would never be paroled. They would spend all their years in the institution. Others would, theoretically, emerge healthy-minded, stable persons.

California is one of several states experimenting with such an institution. It is implemented by a Sexual Psychopath Law.[1] According to the statute, a sexual psychopath is:

any person who is affected in a form predisposing to the commission of sexual offenses, and in a degree constituting him a menace to the health or safety of others, with any of the following conditions:
(a) Mental disease or disorder

[1] *State of California, Welfare and Institutions Code*, Sec. 5500–19,

(*b*) Psychopathic personality

(*c*) Marked departures from normal mentality

Where there is reason to believe a convicted defendant may be a sexual psychopath, the court causes a hearing to be held in the matter. Psychiatrists examine the defendant, and if he is certified a sexual psychopath, the judge orders him placed in a state mental institution for an observation period not exceeding ninety days. If the superintendent of the hospital confirms the earlier diagnosis, but states the patient would not benefit from care and treatment in a state hospital, and is a menace to the health and safety of others, "the court shall then cause the person to be returned to the court . . . to await further action with reference to such criminal charge." That is, a conventional criminal sentence will be imposed or the court will "make such other suitable disposition" as it deems necessary.

But if the hospital superintendent reports that the individual would benefit from a state hospital stay, the court is directed by law to commit him for "an indeterminate period." [2] This is not an indeterminate penal sentence. The judge merely holds up final disposition regarding the conviction, making it possible to keep the patient in hospital for whatever period is required. The action is more on the order of the suspended sentence, for the imposition of that sentence has not taken place.

The individual is the beneficiary of a very advanced program of treatment in the hospital. It includes individual and group therapy, in what is conceived of as "a therapeutic community." In the hospital patients are considered as people; they are accepted, not rejected by staff. They are treated as sick people, not criminals.

Only if the superintendent certifies a patient has recovered emotional stability and is cured of his ailment will that person be eligible for return to the free community. He is then sent

[2] Atascadero State Hospital has been designated the treatment center for sexual psychopaths committed in California.

back to court. The judge makes final adjudication. In practice, this means the sentence is imposed, suspended, and the defendant placed on probation. The law specifies the probation term must not be less than five years.

This program has been in existence too short a time to allow for valid follow-up study. However, if later research indicates the program is successful, from the standpoint both of community protection and of individual treatment, there will undoubtedly be expansion of the idea. Other states will take it up. Perhaps categories other than sex offenders will be included.

Group Therapy

We have noted the trend to group therapy in institutions. A number of states are experimenting with the technique. Exciting reports have come out. Group therapy programs, economical both in cost and time, will be developed in an increasing number of settings in the near future. There have been some attempts at introducing such treatment into parole and probation agencies, with inconclusive results to date, partly because professional leadership has not been provided, the therapy being attempted by probation and parole officers.

Group Counseling

What may be termed "group counseling," to differentiate it from professional group therapy, is a fairly new concept in correctional service, particularly in institutions. There are two types of group counseling.

In one, all institutional personnel, from custodial officers to wardens, are trained in simple group counseling techniques. Thus, a shop instructor or an officer on yard duty will work with small groups. Counseling goes on everywhere, as occasion demands, at work and at play. Every member of the staff is expected to take part. This conception of counseling has been developed with reported good results in the California State Prison at Soledad and elsewhere.

The second type of group counseling is conducted exclusively by and for the persons with problems. There is no professional or staff leadership whatever. For certain emotional difficulties this approach appears superior to professional group therapy. However, it does not need to be undertaken to the exclusion of the latter.

For instance, within an institution there may be a professionally led group therapy program and a unit of an organization such as Alcoholics Anonymous, which is the outstanding example of a nonprofessional group counseling medium. In A.A., alcoholic works with alcoholic on mutual problems. Few would deny that A.A. produces results *because* the alcoholic will listen to another alcoholic before he will give a respectful hearing to a nonalcoholic professional therapist.

The general pattern of A.A. has been applied to the treatment of other problems. Narcotics Anonymous, as we have seen, is based on the same philosophy and approach. At California's Atascadero State Hospital, sexual psychopaths operate their own Emotional Security Program, on practically the same basis. They work with each other on their emotional conflicts and ailments. The halls are decorated with the slogan: YOU CAN GROW UP AND GO HOME. Emotional maturity brings emotional security, patients learn. They try to grow up, with each other's help. When they go out on probation, they are eligible to attend meetings of another nonprofessional group therapy organization, the Emotional Maturity Program.

Some thought has been given to the formation of something like this for probationers and parolees. Such efforts as have been made to implement the idea have been sporadic and not too successful, perhaps partly because probation and parole officers have been involved, and this tends to vitiate the principle of person-with-problem helping person-with-problem. More attention will perhaps be given in future to experimenting with the mutual aid program without official leadership.

Biochemistry

An exhilarating chapter of medical history is being written in the field of biochemistry. Some decades ago, medical men gave intensive study to the role of the endocrines. We know now that they have a good deal to do with motivating behavior. The malfunctioning of glands can account for bizarre, even criminal, conduct. We also have learned that chemicals can correct some glandular conditions which produce discomfort and erratic activity. The hyperthyroid person, quick to overreact, to become hysterical, can have his condition alleviated.

In the mental diseases, biochemistry, only yesterday, produced tranquilizing drugs which make manic patients accessible for treatment. University of Oregon scientists recently reported synthetic hormone compounds believed capable of controlling the urges of homosexuals and sex deviates without reducing potency.

A vast field lies before us. Biochemical approaches to treatment of behavior difficulties seem almost limitless. Crime and delinquency are behavior difficulties. The public will probably support biochemical research where it would not favor investigation of delinquency and crime, although both would travel in the same direction. Biochemistry may produce a radical reorientation of criminology, penology, and casework.

New-Style Penal Colony?

The term "penal colony" sends a shudder through us, for we associate it with abominations like Devil's Island. Yet, have we thoroughly explored the possibilities of using decent colonies as a treatment setting?

Consider a few of the many reasons why the conventional

prison fails. At best, under the finest leadership, with optimum staff and equipment, it remains an abnormal place in which to live. It cannot be otherwise. The inmate has lost that precious possession of the free individual—personal liberty. He has been deprived of his family, of normal love and affection. He must either suspend sexual and other affectional behavior or engage in what society defines as abnormal conduct in that area. The prisoner is also denied what every mature person must have in order to maintain his self-respect: he has been denied the right to make his own decisions and to take responsibility for those decisions. He arises according to rule, eats, works, bathes, plays, washes his hands, sleeps, according to regulation. When he walks across the yard, he must have a pass. He goes through corridors to the accompaniment of clanging steel gates and the scrutiny of turnkeys. He is constantly reminded he is less than a man; for he not only is not expected to make decisions but is, indeed, forbidden to do so.

Is it likely a person so regimented will emerge a balanced citizen, able to assume his place among his peers, to act for himself, to use good judgment?

Is it not plausible that parolees are handicapped in their struggle to regain status and security by the fact they have been thwarted in institutions, have come out with values more distorted than they were upon admission? (The probationer, of course, often has served a prior penal term as well.)

May it not be that a more normal environment would turn back to society more normal men and women?

Is it not conceivable that a prison colony, new-style, may offer this sort of environment? Recognizing that a great many legal, social, and other factors must be thought through exhaustively before we really know what a colony could or could not accomplish, shall we at least speculate on a hypothetical Utopia for the Disenfranchised?

Suppose one state made a pilot study, setting up an area as

Hometown. It would have rural and urban features; for its residents would come from both types of region, would feel at home only in one or the other. Hometown need not be vast. Perhaps a hundred square miles or less of territory would suffice. There would be homes, factories, farms, stores, shops, churches, parks, playgrounds, schools, police stations, movie houses, all the accouterments of modern life, including television repairmen. Paid personnel, invested with authority by the state, would have over-all control and supervision.

Now let us say that a thousand convicted offenders stand ready for sentence. We would have a thoroughly adequate, no-compromise system for screening out those who would be unsafe risks for Hometown. We would send these to conventional institutions. We would siphon off many others to probation. The remainder would be sent to Hometown—with their families, if the latter chose to go.

The convicted offender would know he is being offered a remarkable opportunity, that he must remain in Hometown at least a specified period, but that his life will be normal.

He and his family arrive. If he is a town dweller, the state, which owns the property, will rent him a house or apartment. If he is a rural man, he will pay rent for lodging and the use of land. The cost will be reasonable, but not much below competitive prices. However, the new arrival may go on a charge account. He will work for wages and pay his way. Since the government pays the wages, and would pay itself back monies owed, the Hometown charge account customer is at least as safe a risk as one who runs up a bill at Saks Fifth Avenue.

So our man starts out in a normal environment, with his family, in a suitable home and job. The children will attend school. The family will go to church together. It will engage in recreation as a family.

Suppose the new citizen of Hometown goes to work in a factory. He will be paid competitive wages. In return, he is expected to work as hard and consistently and fast as would be required outside this special community. How can the state afford such wages? We are assuming, since we postulate Utopia and project our thinking into the future, that these men will be employed in real, not "busy" work. Many will already be union members. They will bring skills with them. They will receive the wages called for anywhere in the state for the given work because we shall have an agreement that if the goods produced in Hometown are not consumed locally, they may be sold on the open market at competitive prices. The rest of the state will be at no disadvantage. Labor will not be undercut. Management will not be underpriced. Thus, the state will pay wages out of the state's earnings. It will plow any profits back into Hometown.

Farm production will be handled in the same way.

If the citizen of Hometown earns more than he needs, he may save it or spend it, as *he* decides (with the usual assist from his wife, no doubt). He and his family do whatever they please, so long as he does his job and does not violate the law. If he has a quarrel with a neighbor, he settles it as he would outside Hometown. If he takes a punch at a co-worker, he will be treated exactly as he would be in any other community. The law will step in when necessary. If he is a good worker, he may be promoted. He might become a foreman, or even the top boss of a plant, the government retaining ownership and general supervision via its full-time personnel.

Professional men would be able to maintain their skills. Under supervision, a doctor, lawyer, dentist, teacher, could follow his profession inside the boundaries of Hometown, even if disbarred outside. What if there be too many doctors? This being a law-abiding profession, oversupply is unlikely, but should that be the case, the Hometown medico would have to find other employment, perhaps as a laboratory technician. Should the law or any other profession become overcrowded, substitute employment would be found for its practitioners. The state, of course, would operate an employment bureau.

Yes, women offenders would be welcome in Hometown. They would bring their families, take their places in business, industry, the professions, homemaking.

Will not convicts leave the jurisdiction of Hometown? Perhaps some will. But if they are properly screened, the risk will be nominal. It is not easy for an entire family to pull up stakes or to escape in a body. Moreover, what is there to escape from? What would the citizen escape to? Only the certainty of being sentenced to a conventional prison term when apprehended, plus an additional term as penalty for escape, plus never again being eligible for Hometown.

So, the offender will know and respect the boundaries of Hometown. They will be well marked. There may be some guard posts.

What about internal discipline? It will operate as elsewhere. There will be courts, jails, police. The citizen may himself be elected to the judiciary. He may work in a jail or serve on the police force. Why not? If he or she has the qualifications, shall we not make use of those talents? Citizenship entails responsibility. We want every citizen to carry responsibilities.

In fact, the government of the community will, for the most part, be carried on by erstwhile offenders. Elective posts will include a mayor and certain administrative officials. Whatever citizen talent is lacking at a given time will be supplied by state employees. A city council, composed of elected residents, will set policy and pass local ordinances. There will, however, be a fairly large corps of paid state officials and other personnel who will constitute a sort of supreme court. They will interpret the basic constitution of Hometown and state laws and regulations having to do with the experimental community. They will see to it that the over-all policy and program are not violated.

If convict members of the community cannot fulfill all the necessary functions, state staff will be depended upon. But so far as possible the offender group will be encouraged to run a fairly self-sustaining community, the official staff remaining in the background. There will always be a hard core of state staff, however, to serve in case of emergency. For example, there will be a fractional but adequate and highly trained fire and police department to supplement the citizen corps. There will be resident physicians, psychiatrists, clinicians, social workers. We shall, of course, have the same problems as in any other community, and professional staff will not be sufficiently available among Hometown's citizens.

Suppose a man or woman has saved some money, wants to go into business for himself? If he or she can stand the competition from inside and outside Hometown, there will be no objection. If the entrepreneur fails, he (she) will receive no special consideration, except that some job will be turned over to him.

May the enterpriser run up bills outside Hometown? Yes, if the firms concerned are apprised of the circumstances.

What if a family has earned enough to buy a car or some other luxury item? Fine! We want all citizens to be adept at driving. We ask only that they obey the law or suffer the normal consequences.

Suppose a man wants to go hunting, or to own a pistol. May he buy and use firearms? Yes, under approximately the same conditions as apply in other parts of the state. Hunting and fishing licenses will be obtainable for applicants who have been carefully screened. Those who need pistols for some reason will require special permits. Hunting and fishing must be done in season and within Hometown's boundaries.

Residents of Hometown may receive visits at any time, from any place. They will want to keep in touch with friends and relatives. If some of these are not so wholesome as they might be, the hope is that life at Hometown will counteract their influence to some extent.

Citizens may make arrangements to leave Hometown on furlough to visit friends and relatives, or to take care of business of one kind or another. Probably the furloughing body will be composed partly of citizens, partly of state staff.

Suppose some businessman wants to set up shop in Hometown, although he is not a resident. May he do so? No. Citizens and the state have a monopoly here. But if neither one nor the other wants to run some sort of enterprise, the state may decide to franchise an outsider.

Will there be bars? Will residents be allowed to drink alcoholic beverages? Certainly! Don't people drink in other communities? Do we want an abnormal environment which will ill prepare a person to re-enter community life elsewhere? Not every resident will want to drink; some will have to quit drinking because it makes trouble for them or others; but those who can drink like ladies and gentlemen will have the right to do so.

Is there not bound to be some trouble in Hometown? Drunkenness? Brawls? Yes, as everywhere. And, as indicated, there will be legal redress for civil and criminal wrongs. And legal punishment for petty offenders. For those who make themselves nuisances or become dangerous, we will have recourse to an echelon of court which will send the offender to a conventional prison outside Hometown, and he will no longer be eligible to return to it. His family will need to move out, too.

If a citizen commits a felony in Hometown, he will be tried in regular criminal court, in the usual manner, and in addition to receiving a new sentence, will be ineligible for Hometown residence again.

How are we going to avoid stigmatizing the families of citizens? Will not children be known as "graduates" of Hometown, pointed at by outsiders? This may be, and here we have one of the toughest problems in the entire scheme. But there is a good chance the problem will resolve itself. Remember, there will be many nonoffenders in the community. One group will merge into the other, so far as identification is concerned. They will all attend the same schools, churches, playgrounds, community centers. In time, there will be intermarriages. More and more the differentiation will amount to less and less. Furthermore, if the experiment is highly successful, there may in the distant future *be* no distinction in the minds of men between a rehabilitated person and one who was never convicted. In that case, would the children be stigmatized?

Would residents pay taxes? Certainly. They would be earning money.

What would happen when the term was served? An official of the state would take official cognizance. The individual and his family could leave at will thereafter.

And if they did not want to leave? Then they would be permitted to remain. This would still further wipe out distinctions between convict and nonconvict population.

The family choosing to remain would have to be self-supporting, of course. It would receive no special help from the state. But it could work for a government agency in the community, or in any of the Hometown enterprises, at going wages.

What would all this cost? Only an expert at cost accounting should attempt an answer to that question. But it would not be surprising if the cost were found to be a great deal less than that of housing inmates in conventional prisons. These Hometowners will work; the cost of their care will be defrayed out of wages; their families will not have to go on relief. Aside from this, think of the millions of dollars saved the state if thousands of Hometowners become so adjusted they never have to be tried again.

Is this a fantastic dream that can never be realized? No. It could be tried in one state. In that manner we would learn what problems are capable of solution, which are not; how practical the scheme is; how beneficial it may be; what the long-term results are for the offender, his family, and the state. After that, if the experiment [3] proves itself, other states might take up the idea. We may at last be able to plow under our prisons.

[3] This proposal is not entirely original. In the 1920s and for an undetermined period thereafter, Russia had its Bolshevo, a prison community for youthful offenders. Convicts were taught trades and presumably paid something for their labor thereafter. But there was no self-government and no private enterprise, nor was an attempt made to create a facsimile of civilian cities, with profit-making recreational facilities, etc. It is believed Bolshevo was abandoned sometime in the 1930s. Other nations, including Mexico, have from time to time experimented with penal colonies of one sort or another.

16

EDUCATION FOR
PROBATION AND PAROLE

We have taken the position that probation and parole are social work undertakings. Not everyone would agree. The sociologist Walter Reckless, for instance, holds that at least these services are not casework. He writes:

I maintain that probation and parole work is probation and parole work and not private agency casework or psychiatric casework. . . . Consequently, the core subject for the training of workers should be courses in probation and parole and not courses in casework.[1]

Professor Class raises some pertinent questions about the training of correctional workers:

In my opinion no reasonable approach to the matter of qualifications can take place until there is a practical, widely agreed on resolution of the question, What is the hard vocational core of probation and parole service? To put its components into logical sequence: (a) Is probation and parole essentially a social work task? (b) Is probation and parole partly social work and partly "something else"? If it is, what specifically is that something else? (c) Is probation and parole generally "something else"? If it is not social work, what is that "something else" in terms of identifiable educational content—law, psychology, sociology, police science, public administration, or some combination of these? . . .

[1] Walter Reckless, "The Controversy about Training," *Focus,* XXVIII (1949), 23.

Certainly . . . without a practical resolution of this question no sound educational planning can take place.[2]

Professor Class would probably agree that probation and parole are social work, and the "something else" is part of social work training, too. Schools of social work recognize that agency functions differ and that specific education for those functions must be added onto the generic.

There is a growing awareness of this. Newman, of the Department of Criminology and Corrections, School of Social Welfare, Florida State University, writes:

The weight of opinion today seems to favor training of the probation counselor in case work with a psychiatric focus. Yet, it stands to reason that preparation in criminology, corrections, and social psychology are vital underpinnings of probation and parole work.[3]

This is saying that generic and specific elements enter into the officer's educational preparation.

The 1956 National Conference on Parole did not go so far as to recommend that field practitioners be graduate social workers. But its workshop on parole staff did hold that for "the more important executive and semi-executive positions an educational background in social work or some related social science field at the graduate school level" was desirable. The workshop further recommended that case supervisors be graduates of social work schools.[4]

That, because of shortages of trained workers, administrators must find a *modus vivendi* is indicated by the position of Richard A. McGee, Director of California's Department of Corrections. The correctional field, he asserts, borrows from

[2] Norman E. Class, "Qualifications: a Realistic Approach to Personnel Requirements," *National Probation and Parole Association Journal*, III (1957), 107.

[3] Charles L. Newman, *Sourcebook on Probation, Parole and Pardons* (Springfield, Ill.: Charles C. Thomas, 1958), p. 73.

[4] Randolph E. Wise, "The 1956 National Conference on Parole," *Federal Probation*, XX, No. 3 (1956), 28–35.

medicine, law, psychology, social work, and other areas. It is for this reason that some confusion exists concerning professional identification of workers in the field. But so far as the correctional institutions and functions under his leadership are concerned, McGee says, "During the last decade [we] have been looking primarily, but by no means exclusively, to the schools of social work." This is because, "be it an institution or a field service, the correctional agency is concerned with disordered human behavior." [5]

Considering how many fieldworkers are not social work trained, and that they are doing a reasonably effective job on the whole, it would be foolhardy to insist that only social work training graduates a competent probation or parole officer. All that is suggested here is that there is a trend in the direction of recruiting graduates of schools of social work, on the premise they will make better officers. Ernest F. Witte, Executive Director of the Council on Social Work Education, writes:

There are . . . in the *Journal* of the National Probation and Parole Association . . . a good many suggestions which would indicate that the trend is toward a recognition of the validity of social work as the proper preparation for work in the field of corrections.[6]

That this is a trend but not a fact everywhere is clear from the statement by the National Probation and Parole Association on standards for selection of personnel.[7] Here are its suggested minimum qualifications for entering probation and parole work:

1. *Personality*

Emotional maturity, broad common sense, capacity to learn by experience, and a fundamental capacity for and interest in the welfare of human beings are basic and irreplaceable require-

[5] Richard A. McGee, "Professional Education for the Correctional Field," *National Probation and Parole Association Journal,* II (1956), 197.

[6] Letter to the author, February 11, 1958.

[7] *Standards for Selection of Probation and Parole Personnel* (National Probation and Parole Association; undated).

ments for work in the probation and parole field. It goes without saying that such a person must be of good character and balanced personality with special traits of integrity, ability to work with others, an insight into the causes of human behavior, and a general knowledge of his community.

2. *Education*

A bachelor's degree from a college or university of recognized standing, with courses in the social sciences is minimal.

Professional training for probation and parole work in a graduate school of social work maintaining standards acceptable for accredited schools.

3. *Experience*

One year of paid full time experience under supervision in a social welfare agency or similar agency of high standards or one year of graduate work in a recognized school of social work in lieu thereof.

By a "similar agency" is meant one in which such professional work as the following may be done: teaching, personnel work in industry where the applicant did actual adjustment work with individuals and not merely employment service, or casework in an institution or correctional agency.

These suggested standards have been accepted in some places and not in others. In a brochure listing available correctional jobs, the Family Court of Wilmington, Delaware, specified it wanted applicants for the post of probation counselor to have the Master's degree in social work. "Desirable qualifications" for the job of deputy probation officer in St. Paul, Minnesota, included "Master's degree in social work, correctional administration or closely related areas." Madison, Wisconsin, required "two years of graduate social work" of probation and parole agents. Such listings were almost unheard of in the 1930s and 1940s.

On the other hand, the same brochure indicated that Indianapolis would accept the Bachelor's degree as fulfilling its requirement for probation and intake officers, although pointing out that half its staff "have a year or more of graduate social work education." And Brookville, Pennsylvania, looking for a probation and welfare officer, listed no educational qualification whatever and stated, "Experience desirable but not essential."

It is not that some agencies simply are not interested in trained workers (although this may be true here and there). The cold fact is that in some regions such workers simply do not exist, or, if they do, they will not work for the salaries offered under the conditions imposed.

Assuming all the probation and parole agencies in the United States were agreed (as they are not) that they wanted only graduates of schools of social work, they could not begin to be supplied by the graduates of existing educational institutions. If every graduate of every such school in a given year put his sheepskin under his arm and marched into a correctional agency, this still would not fill the need. Subtract from the total number of graduates those who choose to work in other fields (the majority), and a pitiful handful is left for probation and parole. What is the administrator of a correctional organization to do?

He often falls back upon the thinking of the Committee on Personnel Standards and Training of the American Prison Association:

While the graduate curriculum for preservice training is the ideal, it should be recognized that for a long time to come there will be a need for a specific orientation of senior students to the field of corrections. Most correctional institutions and agencies as yet are not in a position to pay salaries and provide the professional climate that would attract graduate trained persons. For some time to come, the senior student is likely to feel more comfortable among the incumbent personnel in most correctional agencies and institutions than is the more highly trained person. The field of correction, in a sense, needs to get confidence in the Bachelor of Arts before it can assimilate too many Masters of Arts.[8]

[8] *Suggested College Curricula as Preparation for Correctional Service* (New York: American Prison Association, 1954), p. 23, quoting Walter C. Reckless, "Training of the Correctional Worker," in Paul W. Tappan, ed., *Contemporary Correction* (New York: McGraw-Hill, 1951) pp. 41–42.

It may seem sad that such a statement could be made *circa* 1954, but its accuracy cannot be contested. Despite progress in the direction of professionalization of the field, it is still true that many workers suspect the educated colleague. That is what the American Prison Association and Reckless were saying in polite language. But as more trained workers are absorbed, they tend, in turn, to absorb the field. Trained social workers are not the "odd balls" they were a couple of decades ago. It is a fact, too, that in a very occasional agency the *un*trained worker is in the minority.

But if probation and parole agencies are to be increasingly staffed by social workers (assuming we agree this is desirable), the field must reach a great many more individuals who, as undergraduates, can be interested in corrections as a career and pointed in the direction of graduate schools. One of the first questions to answer is: How can we inform students there *is* a correctional field? Since becoming associated with college teaching, this writer has been astonished at how many students do *not* know there is a social work field and do *not* know that probation and parole are part of that field. Many of them, in the second semester of their senior year, casting about for a career, suddenly stumble on the facts. Courses in criminology and juvenile delinquency somehow do not include this information. Freshmen orientation courses do not mention probation and parole as possible vocational opportunities.

Correctional administrators must share some of the responsibility for this state of affairs. They have overlooked a great opportunity, for the most part. They have not told their story in educational circles, have not seen to it that corrections find a place in vocational planning courses.

But if we should have a great many more students who, with a baccalaureate, wanted to enter graduate schools of social work to prepare for careers in correctional organizations, where would we find enough schools? All together, as at present organized, they cannot turn out enough trained workers to satisfy the need in the social work field as a whole. We shall need more graduate schools. And all of them will need to accept the fact that correctional services are social work; that training for them is the province of the social work school; and that it is possible to practice professional social work in correctional settings.

The battle over standards has not been localized in the field alone. Some correctional workers resist the idea of professionalization. But some teachers in social work schools deny they have a responsibility to train and educate correctional workers.

There has been more reluctance to accept this responsibility in the past than there is at present. The arguments were that the correctional setting hampers social work practice; that trained workers are not welcome in correctional agencies anyhow, so why train them?

Faculties are changing their views. The correctional setting is no longer as much a threat to professional practice as heretofore. The field is accepting trained workers, and teachers are agreeing that more students should be prepared for such careers.

Social work educators, in fact, are acknowledging a responsibility to improve the correctional field by furnishing professional employees. The late Kenneth D. Johnson, Dean of the New York School of Social Work, said as much in an article for *Federal Probation*. Social work, he averred, has basic contributions it can make to corrections. And corrections make a contribution to other areas of social work. Corrections "must be restored to social work both because it is an important aspect of the profession's responsibility which has been ignored in recent years and because it can be a source of considerable strength to social work." [9]

[9] Kenneth D. Johnson, "The Role of Social Work Education in Preparing Personnel for the Corrections Field," *Federal Probation*, XX, No. 3 (1956), 58.

Johnson suggested that graduate schools acquaint all of their students with the correctional field. The New York School of Social Work, he said, includes probation and parole case records in generic social work courses. It participates in in-service training programs of correctional agencies. Its curriculum includes material particularly beneficial to those planning careers in corrections. Johnson mentioned a survey of the Council on Social Work Education revealing that eight schools of social work gave the corrections area top priority in their plans for curriculum development. Nineteen more gave it a lesser priority but with "increased interest."

Given enough students interested in correctional work; enough graduate schools; and an acceptance that corrections is part of the social work structure, we will need to study existing curricula to make certain that specific adaptations of generic practice are provided. One of the points of resistance inside the correctional field undoubtedly has to do with the feeling that schools of social work do not provide enough of these specific adaptations. Perhaps we shall want additional courses, in and out of the school of social work: in law, police science, psychology, etc. Corrections, after all, is interdisciplinary, as is all of social work.

A serious impediment to effective staffing is that graduate training is expensive. Despite handsome scholarships, many college graduates cannot afford to stay out of full-time employment another two years in order to earn the Master's degree. And there are workers already in the field, holding the Bachelor's degree, who would like to return to school for graduate training but cannot afford to give up their salaries and take leaves of absence. Is the traditional pattern of graduate training, with daytime field work and daytime classes, to be conceived of as immutable? We are crying for workers, throughout the social work field, yet have not seen our way clear to make it possible for more students to get training. Would standards inevitably suffer if classes were offered at night, so that part-time and even full-time workers could matriculate? Would the student receive a second-class supervised field training experience if social agencies gave such training evenings as well as by day? Much of the social work function can be performed at night; in fact, some of it can be done better in the evening than by day. Does the social agency have an obligation to the field as a whole to furnish evening internships? These are questions which cannot be answered without further thought and study. But they will have to be answered if we are to meet the demand for workers as it exists today and as it will continue for many years to come.

Dean Johnson described a work-study plan at the New York School of Social Work which is at least a first step in the direction indicated. It is geared to the needs of workers already in the field. The plan involves an increase in the number of part-time credits allowable toward the degree. It calls for full-time study during the winter and spring semesters; also in the summer, in one field-work setting; and completion of courses or project on a part-time basis. No change in degree requirements is provided. The plan still requires one year of campus residence with field work, plus a summer of field experience, it will be noted.

Because social work schools have up to now not turned out enough graduates to fill the need, there has been a move in the direction of providing preprofessional social welfare curricula at the undergraduate level. Also, there have developed a number of undergraduate departments, not identified with social work as such, which offer courses that are called "correctional curricula" and the like. There has been much argumentation and considerable misunderstanding about this, particularly as to what such curricula can legitimately offer without lowering standards in the field.

Those who see possibilities in such curricula assert:

So long as certain agencies, notably in public assistance, corrections, and group work, cannot get optimum staff through
the graduate schools, it is desirable, and next best, to seek
them at a lower level.

An undergraduate social welfare major would accomplish
two desirable objectives. It would prepare students to enter
graduate schools; and it would orient those going directly into
the field with a Bachelor's degree. If holders of the baccalaureate are *ipso facto* eligible for appointment, is it not prefer-
able that they have some orientation to the field they are entering? Is not a major in social welfare more valuable to such
students than one in physical education or chemistry or home
economics?

Those who oppose the idea of undergraduate curricula offer
this critique:

To give any kind of social work orientation and training
at the undergraduate level is a disservice to the field of social
work, for it has the effect of lowering standards which the field
has been fighting for generations to raise and maintain. Some
concede that an undergraduate student might profitably take
a course like "The Field of Social Welfare," to give him a cross-
section view, but that would be for the purpose of better preparing him for the graduate school.

An undergraduate is unprepared for methods courses. He
cannot intern in a social agency. Without such field placement
he will not get the training essential to later practice. It is impossible to transmit skills by classroom method alone.

To graduate people with a baccalaureate who have the impression that they are social workers is a disservice to student
and agency alike.

Whatever position the reader takes, he will agree that these
issues must be faced and worked out, one way or another,
if we are to have guides for the education of probation and
parole officers.

The next decade will probably see a trend toward some kind of preprofessional education. The writer believes it will, at a minimum, be based on these propositions:

1. Undergraduate preparation can serve the field of social work by enlisting interest on the part of students seeking careers.

2. It can better prepare those who will seek admission to graduate schools of social work.

3. It can furnish orientation that will be of some little benefit to those who must enter social work with only a Bachelor's degree, and this seems inevitable so long as graduate schools do not turn out enough workers.

4. Some courses, at present at the graduate level, probably can be taught as effectively at the undergraduate level, freeing graduate time for other work. "The Field of Social Welfare" and "Social Legislation" are two that come to mind in this connection.

5. The undergraduate curriculum will always want to emphasize the desirability of a broad liberal education as the base for later professional education. Most of the undergraduate major, in fact, will be devoted to this, with only a limited number of offerings which can be called "social welfare content" courses.

6. Informational material can be communicated in a classroom, but skills are learned by supervised practice only.

7. The undergraduate curriculum should not lead students to believe they will graduate as caseworkers, group workers, or community organization workers. Students should be given to understand clearly and unequivocally what the curriculum can and cannot do for them. They should realize that only an internship such as at present is offered by graduate schools will make skilled practitioners of them. "Field experience" and "field observation" courses, occasionally given in undergraduate years, are no substitutes for a real internship.

8. An undergraduate major in social welfare is something distinct. It is not sociology, psychology, public administration, or general social science. It is social science and biological science and humanities and "something else." The something else is a small group of content courses intended to communicate social welfare knowledge and orientation.

17

OTHER ADMINISTRATIVE
CONSIDERATIONS

Other administrative problems require a word.

Recruitment and Retention of Staff

The majority of correctional agencies do not recruit through a merit system, although the trend is in that direction. Civil service and other merit systems offer no panaceas in recruitment. They tend to overprotect the mediocre and average and to offer insufficient opportunity for advancement to the above-average worker. Nevertheless, they are superior to a system of recruitment via the spoils system.

If we do provide a merit system, examinations all too often fail to measure the qualities and abilities we seek in the officer. How are we going to get a realistic evaluation of character and personality? Will either a written or an oral examination assure this? Even knowledge of the field, while more measurable, is difficult to reduce to a score based upon examination of the applicant. And when opinion, point of view, breadth of vision, are being plumbed, the difficulties in measurement are practically insuperable. An intelligent testee can guess what is wanted and give it as his own.

Merit systems, however, are refining their processes, and the past ten years have seen some improvement.

Once they are recruited, we want to keep competent staff

members. However, turnover is high. There are a number of reasons: worker and job were not meant for each other to begin with; salaries are not what they should be; promotional opportunities are meager; working conditions are unsatisfactory.

The Council on Social Work Education, through a Subcommittee on Supply of Social Work Personnel for Corrections, made a comprehensive report on employment practices in the field.[1] Seventy-nine correctional agencies, out of 202 queried, responded to a questionnaire on the subject. Perhaps the fact that such a small proportion did respond indicates they are an atypical group, more than ordinarily interested in promoting high standards of performance. Therefore, inferences cannot be drawn for the field as a whole, in the opinion of the subcommittee. Of the respondent agencies, 34 reported they had not changed their educational requirements in the five years prior to 1956, while 31 had raised them and 8 lowered them. Six did not answer the question.

Graduate training was preferred for 85 percent of the probation and parole officer positions.

An official merit system served 40 agencies, a voluntary merit system was available to 32, and 5 had no merit system. Two agencies did not respond to the item on the questionnaire.

Six hundred and sixty-five positions had been filled with persons who met the preferred standard (one or two years of graduate work); 901 met the minimum standard (usually less than graduate level) but not the maximum; while 38 had not met the minimum.

A total of 1,669 persons had been employed during the study period, with 129 vacancies still in existence at the time. This indicates a high turnover after recruitment.

Only 6 out of 29 agencies reported no problem in filling positions with graduate-trained personnel.

[1] *Social Work Education,* Vol. V (1957); special recruitment issue.

Some reasons for recruitment and retention problems, as cited in the study were: low salaries; lack of interest in the correctional field on the part of graduate social workers; uncertain advancement opportunities; high caseloads. The contributing factor most frequently advanced was of noncompetitive salaries. Other points were noted: difficult working conditions; inadequacies of supervision; lack of tenure; absence of retirement benefits; inability of social work graduates to adjust to the correctional setting.

Salaries

What about salaries? We have a fairly recent statement on the situation in parole.[2] In 1956 William L. Jacks queried agencies in each state as to annual salaries of parole officers. The average minimum was $3,946; the average maximum, $4,776 —a sorry picture for these times. Minimum salaries ranged from a low of $2,880 to a high of $5,054. The range of maximum salaries ran from a low of $3,000 to a high of $6,360. Connecticut had the distinction of offering the $6,360 figure. Kentucky had the lowest minimum—$2,880 a year. Even the maximums would compare unfavorably with salaries in such occupational categories as locomotive engineer, plumber, and long-distance trucker. And while social work salaries as a whole would be at a similar disadvantage, the bleak fact remains that if the profession intends to adhere to expressed standards of recruitment and operation, ways will have to be found to make social work more attractive financially. Even social workers eat.

Caseloads

What about caseloads, one of the reasons why workers abandon the field? All past studies have shown that only a tiny

[2] William L. Jacks, *A Comparison of Parole Agents' Salaries, Caseloads, and Supervision Duties* (mimeographed, 1957), quoted in Charles L. Newman, *Sourcebook on Probation, Parole and Pardons* (Springfield, Ill.: Charles C. Thomas, 1958), pp. 211–18.

proportion of organizations have workable caseloads. The bulk of probation and parole agencies frankly admit they place upon the worker a load so great as to make casework treatment difficult in the extreme, if not impossible. Jacks [3] had something on this, too. In South Carolina, parole caseload averaged 313.6 per agent in 1956. Lowest loads were in Delaware, Kentucky, and Wisconsin, averaging 50 cases, a workable number. New York averaged 80.2 cases; California, 92. If we figure that the maximum number of cases an officer can carry efficiently is about 50, only three states are in this category. If we set the top limit at 75, then fifteen states fall in the class. Thirteen states showed loads above 100.

The public, legislators, and others concerned with budgets must be helped to understand that an agency gets what it pays for, and so does the citizenry. It is economical to staff adequately. There are reasons to believe it costs the public more to apprehend and retry recidivists than it would to staff properly and supervise effectively.

The Law Enforcement Function

One of the most persistent debates in the corrections field has to do with how far the probation and parole officer should go in performing the law enforcement function with which he is charged. No one denies he is so charged. Few would have him altogether forget he has such function in law. The argument is over what this means by way of administrative policy. Just how much surveillance should officers undertake? Should they make arrests? Carry arms? Use handcuffs? Some say "yes"; some, "no"; some, "maybe"; some, "sometime."

Ervis Lester, of the California Adult Authority, looks at it this way: parole supervision is a two-sided endeavor—surveillance and treatment. "The surveillance aspect connotes a close, watchful scrutiny of the parolee's conduct with power

[3] *Ibid.*

to arrest and detain. The treatment side suggests professional guidance in meeting everyday problems as well as emergencies." [4] Which of these phases should dominate the work and philosophy of the parole officer, asks Lester. He agrees that some amount of surveillance there must be. But he points out that "the usual reaction of parolees to surveillance is one of fear and distrust." It is his personal belief that:

Fear of consequences is of small value in helping a parolee steer a true course. Fear is a negative factor and, as such, it has little if any influence upon the parolee who is full of hope and whose efforts are winning social and economic acceptance in his community.[5]

On the other hand, for the person who is slipping, who begins to feel frustrated, fear is already present. "Surely it is not more fear that is needed—rather it is hope that might conceivably turn the tide." [6] Consequently, Lester suggests, the positive treatment aspect should receive the greater emphasis.

The author believes that most thoughtful workers will agree with Lester, in general. We prefer to use the constructive treatment approach. It *is*, in most situations, more effective than the fear-inspiring technique. But we have not, by saying this, squarely faced up to all aspects of the question. Should or should not the officer, *when* indicated, do surveillance work? When *is* it indicated? What *are* all the law enforcement functions of the officer? Are they different for juveniles than for adults?

Barnes and Teeters come out flatly for an officer who is unencumbered by law enforcement obligations: "Supervision does not mean espionage; the parole officer must not be a policeman. He should be a friend in need, an advisor." [7]

[4] Ervis W. Lester, "Parole Treatment and Surveillance—Which Should Dominate?" in *Proceedings, 82nd Annual Congress of Correction, 1952,* pp. 53–56, reprinted in Newman, *op. cit.,* p. 264.

[5] *Ibid.,* p. 266.   [6] *Ibid.*

[7] Harry Elmer Barnes and Negley K. Teeters, *New Horizons in Criminology* (New York: Prentice-Hall, 1951), p. 791.

It is the opinion of the present writer that few persons who have had field experience would agree completely with this postulate. It may seem plausible to the academician, but the man who handles probationers or parolees daily would very likely agree in the main with Lester and not with Barnes and Teeters. He would probably say, "It would be nice not to *have* to invoke my law enforcement powers. But, unfortunately, I cannot avoid this in some cases. And when it needs doing, it must be done, and I would be derelict in my duty if I did not do it." Administrators cannot blink the fact that their agencies are charged with community protection. They are expected to eliminate from their caseloads individuals who are obvious and immediate hazards. They cannot reject the fact that officers take an oath to enforce the law.

This does not argue an all-out, billy-swinging, gun-toting approach. Rather, it calls for some interpretation. Let us return to the Barnes and Teeters statement. What do we mean by "espionage," which those authors assert supervision is *not?* It can mean various things. But if by it we mean investigation of facts, then supervision would appear definitely to involve such. Giving it an ugly name does not countervail the fact that many noncorrectional as well as correctional agencies investigate. The public assistance agency does. Child welfare agencies do. Adoption agencies do. Foster home placement agencies do. Medical social workers investigate. Is not the probation or parole officer properly charged with investigating what the individual under his supervision is doing? Social workers would say he is. They would not gag at the idea. They would say such "espionage" need not vitiate the casework function, although it would if ineptly handled.

The parole officer, say Barnes and Teeters, should not be a policeman. What law, in what state, specifies that a probation or parole officer should be a policeman? None. He is a peace officer but not a policeman. Every policeman is a peace officer, but not every peace officer is a policeman. The correctional worker's peace officer functions are not precisely and altogether those of a policeman, and to say so is to set up a straw man with the intention of demolishing him.

Should the officer be a friend in need, an advisor? Yes, indeed! Who would disagree? But does this mean he cannot at the same time be alert to danger signals, to potential recidivism? Probation and parole officers may be credited with the ability to do both.

To summarize:

Every probation and parole officer has some responsibility for community protection.

He hopes he will not have to emphasize this function in a given case, but recognizes this is inevitable at times.

His emphasis is upon treatment, but that involves investigation of the behavior of his charges. He could not treat intelligently without some amount of investigation.

He hopes so to treat that he will not have to invoke his law enforcement powers.

But when that becomes necessary in the public interest, he will do so.

He knows he must individualize, in surveillance as well as in treatment of another kind. Some persons require practically no field check. Others require close investigation.

The aim of probation and parole, with adult or juvenile, male or female, is so to help the individual that he no longer wants to harm society. When that time comes—and it often does—the law enforcement function becomes quiescent. Until then, realistic administrative considerations dictate that this function be not relegated to the scrap heap. The public would eventually rise up against such administration and tear down the good with the bad.

Public Relations

This brings us to another matter—the building of good public relations.

The writer queried 1,450 individuals by questionnaire as to their beliefs about probation and parole. They were, with the exception of 4 percent of the sample, college juniors and seniors majoring in the social sciences, over half of them planning to enter social work. The 4 percent consisted of adults taking courses in police science, all of them in police work. This represented a far from typical sample of the general population. What makes the responses interesting is the very degree of selectivity. Here were informed, intelligent people, most of them sympathetically inclined toward any social work endeavor. Some were engaged in police work and from that vantage point held opinions based upon observation and actual field experience.

The group was asked to indicate whether a given proposition was true or false. If a respondent had no opinion, he left the item blank.

A total of 57 percent marked as true the statement: "Most parole systems are inefficiently operated." Seventy-five percent believed most parole systems are influenced by politics in at least some of their operations; 41 percent thought "most adult probationers commit new crimes while on probation"; 37 percent said the same about parolees; 56 percent believed most probation systems are inefficiently operated; 70 percent said most probation systems are influenced by politics in at least some of their operation; and 19 percent believed that most crimes were committed by parolees or probationers.

Judgments of police officers were, on the whole, harsher than those of the civilian students.

This special kind of public believed certain things about probation and parole—largely uncomplimentary. Evidence establishes these opinions are unsound. How is it we have not been able to illuminate such issues more effectively?

The correctional field has not been spectacularly skillful in public relations. Social workers have the same shortcoming generally. Schoolteachers, formerly quite ineffectual in this area of endeavor, have improved their public relations, and this has been due in no small measure to the fact they employed professional public relations workers and undertook a calculated, long-range program of public education.

Probation and parole have something their practitioners believe worth while. That something needs to be explained so the public understands and approves. The correctional field has an obligation to inform the public honestly, fairly, and lucidly, through the use of professional public relations techniques and workers. The correctional worker need not feel ashamed of his practice. He can be proud of some of the attainments of probation and parole. Telling the story takes professional know-how.

The public is entitled to know. Given the facts, it will increasingly accept these services, for they will be recognized as in the interest of the public weal.

INDEX

Absconding, of probationer, 41; of juvenile probationer, 43; of parolee, 69 f.

Acceptance, of offender by correctional worker, 137

Administration, separation from policy formation, 58 f.; problems, 231-39

Adult, *see* Offender, adult

Adult Authority, California, 58 f., 66, 113, 234

Agencies, social work: types of, 81; functions and limits, 141 f.; referral to, 158; rules essential to, 171; investigation by, 236 f.

Agency, parole-granting, 64-67

Aggression, and crime, 99 f.

Alabama, 34

Alaska, 27n

Alcohol, *see* Intoxicants

Alcoholics Anonymous, attitude toward drinking, 191; group counseling medium, 209

Ambivalence, 145 f.

American Law Institute, Model Youth Correction Act, 57

American Prison Association, Committee on Personnel Standards and Training, 223

Antisocial attitudes, of probationers and parolees, 78 ff.

Applicability, of probation, 29-32

Aptekar, Herbert H., dynamic approach, 134

Army, group therapy, 166

Arrest, notification of, by ex-offender, 195

Arrival report, 69, 178 f.

Associates, undesirable, 40, 142; rule re, 192 f.

Asthenic type, and crime, 90

Atascadero State Hospital, Emotional Security Program, 209

Athletic type, and crime, 90

Augustus, John, "father" of probation, 11 ff.; career, 13 ff.; critics of, 17 f.

Australia, penal colonies, 46 ff.

Authority, value of, in aid to juvenile, 16, 161; acceptance of, by client, 139 ff.; as casework tool, 139-41; resentment of, 169; value of, in casework, 171-99; enforcement of stated rules, 173

Automobile, regulations on owning and operating of, 189 f.

Autonomy, local: and centralized probation administration, 28

Bail, 10; for children, 16 f.

Baltimore, Md., study of overcrowded areas, 99

Banay, Ralph S., on aggression, 100

Barnes, Harry Elmer, and Negley K. Teeters, on function of parole officer, 235 f.

Barron, Milton L., on causes of delinquency, 86n

Beard, Belle Boone, study of children on probation, 201

Beccaria, Cesare B., philosophy of criminology, 3 f.

Behavior, motivation, 2, 100 f., 145, 159 f.; affected by physical condition, 93 f., 210; effect of environment on, 94-99; and personality, 126 f.; affected by childhood experiences, 144; ambivalence in, 145 f.; modification of, through group therapy, 166 f.

Benefit of clergy, 6 f.

David Dressler believes that those who work in probation and parole should be trained in social work. This is one considered opinion that is contained in an informed account of correctional work in the United States.

Lending weight to the argument that crime is the concern of society, he presents a brief survey of probation and parole — its statutes, rules, and procedures. He shows different opinions on important aspects of correction—such as "causes" of crime and delinquency, attitudes toward the offender, the two-fold obligation of community protection and individual treatment. He discusses probation and parole in reference to both juveniles and adults.

Dr. Dressler's own points of view emerge, supported by a wealth of case material: first, that criminals are individuals and can be treated only as such; that probation and parole officers can most efficiently perform their work when they have been schooled in social work and have the tools of psychology, sociology, practical experience in interviewing and in evaluating personality. He has much to say about the role and capacity of probation and parole officers which will be useful to those in correctional work.

Of special interest is his proposal for a prison community in